# RHYTHM OF RAGE

## "Story of Naima X"

*by*

DENISE P. FORD

To Contact the Author:
P.O. Box 88501
Carol Stream, IL 60188
www.reflectionsofgrace.net

ISBN: 1-4196-9753-6

ISBN-13: 9781419697531

Visit www.booksurge.com to order additional copies.

DISCLAIMER

This is a work of non-fiction. However, to protect the author and to prevent defamation of character to any individual, the names of characters and companies have been changed.

# TABLE OF CONTENTS

# INTRODUCTION

We all walk down different paths in life. Whatever the path, there isn't one soul immune from life's troubles. Along the way what hurts us most is the fact that we are selfish human beings. Often we don't freely love or care about the safety and well-being of others unless we have an ulterior motive.

But sometimes you have experiences and learn lessons that make you want to share and pass down your wisdom to help others along this journey called life. You realize that if it were not for the Lord, you would not be here. Your life experiences are your testimony.

I've come to believe that I don't need to have a label or title to be someone. I've learned that whatever a person overcomes can make them extraordinary. When I was going through my worst in life, I felt ashamed and defeated. I felt deeply wounded, and I became good at hiding my scars. In order to be accepted, I learned to wear a mask. When I walked away from my marriage, the cords of love, laughter, hurt, pain, betrayal, and deception revealed this mask of sorrow. Since then I've had a chance to reflect and move forward. I no longer try to fit in with others, compete, or perceive myself as broken, depressed, and angry. My prayers and years of self-therapy have given me the assurance that God is listening.

I am on a new path that has transitioned my life's purpose into a spiritual calling. If it had not been for this divine intervention, I would still be running around in the dark. It's easy to put the blame on others when we fail or fall short. But sometimes when bad things happen to us, it opens the door to new opportunities. I was taught to be kind to others, and that I would receive kindness in return. But that wasn't the experience I had in the majority of my circumstances. I've learned to be kind anyway. I've learned to forgive by surrendering and releasing the tears; thus, allowing time to change my perception. Forgiveness is very powerful, and it is the key to unlocking the doors to many blessings. I believe that if you subscribe to this way of thinking, one day you, too, will start to reap things in your life.

The most important thing that I can share with you, no matter what road you have to travel to find your life's purpose, is that God will be with you. Remember whatever happens, it's not about you. It's about God. He will turn all your sad days into sunny ones and turn your night into day.

I have been inspired by God to write this story as a living testimony to show how merciful and good He is to all those who believe. Along this journey, I have faced the unthinkable and the unforgettable. Somehow, though, there seemed to be a light shining brightly, waiting for me. In search of love and protection, I have only come to find that there is nowhere to turn but to that light, God.

Many people will cross or even travel along your path. Some will be patient and positive in helping you find your way. Others will bring negativity that will cause you to fall or go astray. There will be all kinds of distractions to hinder you. The road will have stumbling blocks, U-turns, and hard bumps. There will be rain, storms, and challenges. You will need an insurance card called "faith" to get you through the darkest times. The light that shines ahead of you is Jesus directing the way. Continue to stay on His path until you reach your destination.

*I dedicate this book in loving memory to my grandfather, the late Bishop Ceasar A. Ford.*

"OWE NO ONE ANYTHING EXCEPT TO LOVE ONE ANOTHER: FOR HE WHO LOVES ANOTHER HAS FULFILLED THE LAW."

**Romans 13:8**

# STORY OF NAIMA X

A name is special to the soul as it connects the spirit to its divine purpose. *Naima*'s origin is Arabic, meaning "content, happy," which is from na'ima: "to live in comfort, to be worry-free."

"FOR YOU FORMED MY INWARD PARTS: YOU COVERED ME IN MY MOTHER'S WOMB. I WILL PRAISE YOU, FOR I AM FEARFULLY AND WONDERFULLY MADE. MARVELOUS ARE YOUR WORKS, AND THAT MY SOUL KNOWS VERY WELL."

**Psalms 139:13-14**

# Detroit - 1966

## CHAPTER 1

Every soul has been given an assignment before the foundations of the earth. Sometimes an assignment can entail different phases of unfortunate circumstances resulting in anger and escalating into rage like mine. For a long time, I had no idea that prior to my existence, the Lord had predestined the steps I would take. The angels were preparing for the plans God has bestowed upon my life.

A chorus of sparrows flew towards the East as the wind blew in early spring of 1966 when I was born into the lives of Bunny Harris and Jonathan A. Wakefield, Jr. of Detroit—known as the "Motor City." When I was a little girl, my father would tell me stories about my infancy. I remember listening to him tell of the time my mother left me at the hospital because she didn't want me. As soon as my father heard the news, he came running to my rescue.

Another time, after arriving home to a cold house, my parents placed me inside a blanket and put me in front of the heater vent. While they both drifted into a deep sleep, the heater burned me to the point that I awakened them with the screams of an innocent soul. I was burned on my left thigh, causing swelling around the size of an orange. My father immediately put some compression on the leg to take some of the swelling away, and then he rushed me to the hospital. I can't remember the pain, and for that I thank God. But I am always reminded of this story when I look at my thigh. I'm still very self-conscious of it, especially when I wear shorts.

My father and mother apparently couldn't work things out to remain together, so my father eventually left. I remember him coming to visit from time to time. My two older brothers lived with us at this time, and my mother treated my brother Lionel like a charm. Rocky, the oldest, and I didn't get the same treatment. I remember my mother calling me names like *heifer* and *wench*, which hurt my feelings. I was always trying to stay in my brothers' shadows because I was afraid to be alone with her. My father eventually told me that my mother hadn't wanted any girls. I vaguely remember the conversation. She had resented being pregnant after she found out I was a girl. She even lit a cigarette to her stomach to cause physical pain to herself. While he expressed my mother's behavior, I could also hear her voice when she would berate my father's trifling ways. Somehow I believed that he wanted me to resent her.

When I turned five years old, I started kindergarten. I would walk to school with Lionel every day, and we usually stopped off at a particular bar on our way to beg for money from all kinds of strangers. Then we would run to the candy store to buy "Now & Laters," "skins," cakes, and pop. I have no idea what time we would get to school, but Lionel was always responsible for me. And he knew that I depended on him. Sometimes he'd abuse that power and tease me by threatening to run off, so I learned quickly to find ways to please him, like offering him my dinner at suppertime. He only wanted my chicken or the meat on my plate.

I don't recall seeing my mother going to work, but she was always out attending to business. When Jonathan came to visit we would be so happy because he would bring us goodies and give us money. When he put me on his lap, I would kiss and hug him until his rough beard scratched my face.

In between my father's visits, I would try to do what I was told by my mother and brothers. When Rocky babysat us, he'd get into fights with Lionel. And one of them always ended up with a bloody nose. Lionel and I suffered serious abuse from Rocky. He made us drink buttermilk, which I didn't like anyway, from a dirty metal pipe, and then he yelled at us. The taste was awful and disgusting. He was always pulling pranks and laughing afterwards. Lionel and I were tormented! But Rocky had a weakness: his stuttering problem. So when he was too mean to us, we teased him. That was our way of making him feel bad.

One day I realized that we all had different last names. My mother told me then that my father wasn't Jonathan Wakefield, the man I had adored growing up. She told me my father was Henri Davis. I recalled seeing another man visiting when I was younger, but I had never called him Daddy or remembered showing him any affection. He'd never talked to me or bought me anything. My brothers adored Jonathan and called him Daddy, which was why I saw him as my father, too. He didn't treat us differently. He would embrace all of us with jokes, love, and goodies.

Some time after Jonathan left, my mother's brother Sammy came to live with us for a little while. This didn't last very long although my mother did try to get along with him. He had a mental problem. They fought a lot, however, and we came home one evening to find that Sammy had cut up our mattresses and ransacked everything. He had a gun in his possession, and we were afraid of him. However, he never mistreated me, and I felt a special bond with him because we shared the same birthday.

Eventually, the police came out to arrest him. When he was incarcerated, we moved because my mother feared that he'd come back to harm us. After leaving our house on Cass Street, we bounced from hotels to motels until my mother felt safe. Then she met Raymond Ham. Raymond worked at Ford Motor Company, and he had a poodle named Cocoa. During the time my mother spent dating him, things got serious. They got married and bought a house on the Eastside of Detroit on Prairie Street.

In between these various men, when my mother was having it hard, she would let us visit our paternal grandparents. So we could see Jonathan for these summers. We fit in because Jonathan had twelve brothers and sisters. They had a lot of kids and lived out in the country in Clinton Township off a dirt road. Being there made my brothers and I feel very safe and loved. Once the summer ended my mother would come pick us up. She would be all dressed up, looking nice and very excited to see us. She always had a can of Colt 45 in her hand. My grandfather was a minister, and he didn't allow people to act out-of-line or be disrespectful. But my mother would talk a whole lot of stuff and brag. She would cuss someone out if they had said something unpleasant to her or gave her a funny look.

My parents never seemed to exhibit true love for each other. They never saw eye-to-eye on anything that I could recall. I later found out that my mother had been accused of stealing Jonathan from her sister, Aunt Kimmy. Aunt Kimmy had been dating Jonathan at the time my mother started sleeping with him. He would sneak my mother out of the house at the age of fourteen and ride her around and have sex with her. He was showing her the fast life, and she ended up pregnant with Rocky and unable to finish high school. This caused a lot of confusion and fighting for years between my mother and her sister, and hate grew between them.

After my mother and Raymond were married, and we arrived at our new home, we were somewhat happy. Our lives did change while living on Prairie Street. I met a really cool friend named Marla. She was cute and very nice to me. My mother gave me a birthday party when I turned eight years old. I invited the friends we had made in school and the neighbors we had gotten to know across the street. I enjoyed dancing the most, and I will never forget dancing the "frog" to the song "Kung Fu Fighting."

For my birthday, I had all kinds of foods and deserts; it was a perfect day in my life! My stepfather was a chef at heart. He did all the cooking in our home from the time we started living with him. We had a two-bedroom house, and I shared the second room with my brothers. Sometimes I would sleepwalk and go outside and stand on the porch. This was dangerous, but I couldn't control it. I also remember peeing in the bed, and my mother fussed and called me names. I felt bad, but I was afraid of the dark after the house settled. Mainly I feared having to crawl out of bed and go to the bathroom during the night. But, I grew out of that fast.

My mother and Raymond seemed happy together at first, but soon they started arguing, really going at each other's throats. Their routine was to go to the liquor store on payday. They would drink Crown Royal and talk. Then the next thing you knew, they were cussing each other out! Things started to change in our happy little home as whatever was causing this unhappiness seemed to progress. My brothers and I learned to stay out of their way. We got used to them fighting like this, but we were scared and unhappy because we never knew what we were coming home to.

Rocky was a teenager at the time, and he got so discouraged that he wouldn't even come home most nights. He found a girlfriend and made some new friends to hang out with. He started bringing home new stuff, too. We had no idea that it was stolen. Lionel was also trying to find a way out, and I was always in my room or on the porch. When the fighting started, I was too scared to go into the house.

Raymond had been in the Army, where he had learned culinary skills and how to use a machine gun. But he was an alcoholic, and he indulged in drinking heavily on the weekends. He had a dangerous temper when he got upset with my mother. Mother would provoke Raymond by accusing him of cheating and lying, and by demanding all his money. She even accused him of looking at me sexually. Raymond believed my mother was ill because of her behavior when she was intoxicated. She loved to argue, and she had to have the last word. And then the violence would start.

But Raymond wasn't all bad. He could really cook some mean chop suey and create other meals out of leftovers. He was an awesome cook; he never messed up a meal. Since he had come into our lives, we had been exposed to all different types of foods. We really did appreciate him in many ways. He provided a nice home and new clothes for school. My mother could not have accomplished this without a man's help. Back then it was harder to be a single parent. She just never seemed happy for any length of time.

Somehow, we made it through the school year. I remember the last day of school. My mother washed my hair and rolled it up for me. Then Lionel and I went outside to play with our friends. We were excited to be out of school and looking forward to sleeping in late during the summer. My mom and Raymond were sitting on the porch drinking and talking. The streetlights came on as it started to get dark, so we didn't play too far away from the front yard. Then I heard Raymond tell my mom to stop talking to him in a very loud and angry tone. But she wouldn't stop talking back, and soon the neighbors could hear them. As I ran across the street to get closer to my mother and see what was happening, she ran and jumped off the porch, screaming at us to get in the car.

We were terrified because we didn't know what was going on. Rocky ran down the street in the direction of his girlfriend's house. I got in the car on the passenger's side, and Lionel dove into the backseat behind my mom. She was trying to find the right key to put into the ignition. She started panicking and crying, and as I looked up at our house I saw Raymond come back outside with his machine gun in his hands. He pulled the trigger. I remember seeing flashes of fire coming straight at us. I heard screams, screeching tires, and *bang bang* noises. I huddled in the seat when the car took off.

My mother stopped at the corner to call our names and see if we could respond, and we answered her, crying. We went to the hospital because Raymond had hit my mother in the head with his fist when she ran out the house. She had to get stitches in the top of her head. Shortly after, she was released from the hospital, and we stayed at a hotel. But somehow we ended up coming back home to Raymond. We were all pretty terrified. Eventually we got the car door fixed where the bullet holes were, but afterwards I never felt safe or the same.

Rocky got word to come back home, too. By this time he had started going out to parties and wearing fancy clothes. He was very handsome, and the girls were always flirting with him. I remember him arguing with my mother the majority of the time. They never had any real conversations, come to think of it. Gradually, he stopped spending time at home with us. His days of babysitting ended, mainly because of the fighting.

Eventually school started back. I remember asking my mother if she would fix my hair on picture day. She said she would get up and press my hair, but when the day came she didn't get out of bed. I was determined to have my picture taken anyway. I put on a rust colored, two-piece pantsuit, and I went to school with my hair looking a mess. The photographer gave me a comb, which didn't do much, but that didn't stop me from taking my picture. When pictures came back, I got teased because my hair wasn't combed. And I had too much Vaseline on my face. My mother was never pleased about my picture.

Finally, my mother broke the news that we were going to move into a bigger house. I guess she and Raymond felt embarrassed after they sobered up. They had a reputation in the neighborhood. Mom said I was going to have my own bedroom this time. I was very excited about it; we got our things packed and moved into our new home in 1974. We had a four-bedroom house on Atkins Street with an upstairs, an attic, and a basement. After we moved, my mother got a job doing something in the medical field. But she didn't hold onto it long. My stepfather was truly the breadwinner.

A neighbor told us about an old couple, who had lived in our house previously. They had been robbed one evening. The husband was murdered in the house, and his blood had stained the walls. After his death, people believed that the house was haunted by his spirit. This terrified me because I believed that there was some truth to this story. It explained some of the noises and weird things that happened while we lived there. Sometimes Cocoa, Raymond's dog, would bark and scratch at the walls in a rage. He'd never behaved like this at the other house. We often heard dishes rattling downstairs while we were upstairs asleep. And one night, the noise got so loud that it woke my mother up. She made Rocky go with her to see where the noise was coming from. They checked all the doors and walked through the basement. Then they discovered that the dishes had been moved around in the dish rack.

While living on Atkins Street, my life was like a fairy tale, or so I thought at first. In the beginning I was excited about having my own bedroom, which was the first room at the top of the stairs. But then I heard about the old man's ghost. Whenever Cocoa, who slept in my room on the floor near my bed, would bark, I would panic. There was never anything visible in the room, however, not even shadows. I used to get so uptight on the weekends because my brothers would spend the night away with their friends. But the older I got, the more confined I was at home. My mother had a leash around my neck; I couldn't even go down the street to visit different girl friends. She never believed in women being friends! When I would pout, she would get worked up and say, "Heifer, you better listen to me, or I will whip your butt." My mother tried to instill fear in me about wanting to have friends. She was so against it, and in time I would find out why. I believe now that she wanted to protect me, but her way of communicating this to me was unclear.

So I learned to create an imaginary life in my room. My favorite toys to play with were Barbie and Ken dolls and my own record player. Sometimes I had play for hours, but there was something missing. And that was a playmate! When I wasn't crying, I would read, write short stories, and journal in my diary. I didn't play much with my dolls or watch a lot of TV. Despite the fact that my mother and Raymond were now sober, the fighting still went on in our home. The weekends were never happy times. I had many fears living with my mother and stepfather. As I got older, my mother got even lazier about combing my hair and making sure my clothes were clean. I wore repeats two and three times a week, and I got teased a lot. No one ever told me I was pretty, so I never thought of myself as being cute. I started doing my own hair, and though I didn't do a very bad job, my hair started to fall out. I think I was combing it too much.

My mother never believed in putting any ponytails or barrettes in my hair. Her favorite hairstyle for me was an Afro, which I hated, as I thought it made me look like a tomboy. I remember one day Raymond said he thought that I was a little boy. This brought tears to my eyes. But my mother persisted in thinking that Raymond was looking at me sexually. She accused him of it often, and she fabricated lies about this issue which made everybody feel uncomfortable living together. None of her accusations were true, but they still made me uncomfortable when I was alone with him. I was always worried about my mother hurting me because of her insecurities concerning my stepfather. She went to the extreme with this jealousy.

Whenever I wanted to be a part of something at school, I knew I had to ask first. I always wanted to join in school activities, and once I asked my mother for money to play the clarinet in the band. She told me we didn't have enough money, and generally she never encouraged me to do anything positive in school. But she was a stickler about my report card. In the second grade I brought home Ds and Fs on my report card, and I knew I was going to get it. So when I got home, I skipped dinner and went to bed. I heard my mother congratulating my brothers on their grades, and then she called me. All I remembered was my hind part burning from an extension cord.



Lionel was eleven, and Rocky was fifteen, I believe. I was around nine years old. One evening, we heard my mother and stepfather downstairs fighting and throwing dishes, moving furniture, and calling each other names. My brothers and I stayed together in Rocky's room, which was upstairs in the far back. It had a balcony with stairs that led to the backyard. Lionel and I were shaking and crying because we didn't know what to do, and Rocky pulled out the Bible and read to us. Trying to comfort us he said, "If it isn't your time to die, then God won't take you." Then we heard our mother screaming, and falling as she tried to come up the stairs. When she called my name, "Naima!" I panicked. I was afraid to answer her—even when she started cussing and demanding that I go to her. Rocky said, "You better go." He unlocked the bedroom door to let me out. I went to the edge of the stairs. My mother saw my shadow and said, "Come here, heifer." When I went to her, she grabbed me and held me in front of her. We were standing halfway up the stairs on the landing, and Raymond was standing downstairs in the middle of the dining room. He was aiming his machine gun at us. Then he pulled the trigger. I could see the fire from the bullets coming straight at us. My mother and I screamed for him to stop. The bullets went by us and ricocheted into the ceiling above our heads. My mother and I ran upstairs to Rocky's room, and we jumped off the balcony to get outside alive. We caught a cab and stayed at a hotel for a day until things cooled off.

Days went by before the damage from the bullet holes was fixed. Rocky begin to speak up, arguing more, and rebelling against our mother. He told her that we were tired of living like this. We were sick of the fighting and her jeopardizing our safety. He was trying to convince mother to leave Raymond. She didn't want to listen, but someone exposed to our schools the environment we were living in. The school started intervening in our home, and my mother knew it was time to make a change.

Another bad fight happened one night, and my mother called the police to warn them. She threatened that she was going to shoot Raymond in self-defense if he came home and tried to harm us. I have no idea what the police said to her, but she hung up the phone and told us to go wait in Rocky's room. When Raymond got home, he tried to use his keys to get inside the house; but my mother yelled through the door for him to leave us alone. He said, "Bunny, I'm going to kill you when I get in!" That's when she realized that he was breaking down the glass door. She ran upstairs and made us escape through the balcony again. We stayed at another hotel, missing school for a few days.

With all of this happening, our grades were dropping, even though we wanted to be at school because it was a safe place. Shortly after that night, my mother asked if we wanted to go live in a home or live together with our pappy's parents. We agreed to live with our grandparents. Our mother and grandparents went to court to relinquish mother's custody to my grandparents. This entitled them to finish caring for us. During the court procedures, my last name was changed to Wakefield and so was Rocky's last name. As I gathered my belongings, I was sad and a little afraid. I knew that my mother didn't want to give us away. I felt she believed that this would be final. I could feel her pain and sense her tears as the days drew near. On the inside I felt relief. I knew that my brothers and I would be safe together—no matter what happened next. We started packing immediately, and we were dropped off in Mt. Clemens.

# CHAPTER 2

We begin living in Mt. Clemens in 1975, and I was approximately nine years old. The transition wasn't difficult for me, but I admit that there were some big changes we had to adjust to and accept. Lionel and I went to Christian Clemens Elementary School, and Rocky went to Mt. Clemens High. We started going to church and learning how to cope in an entirely different environment.

Our new home was above the church where my grandfather preached. It was gray brick with a blue and white sign that read, "Emmanuel Son of Light." We didn't understand church because we had never gone to a real church other than the Catholic Church on Easter. But my grandfather was a Pentecostal pastor who believed in God the Father, Jesus the Son, and being filled with the Holy Spirit. He baptized my brothers and me. He preached to us about Jesus, and he expressed that we needed Him in our lives. We were always reminded of our past, and how God had spared our lives in numerous situations.

That's when I first heard that I had a "testimony." I had no idea what that meant or how to relate it to my current situation, but our grandfather kept us involved in the church to teach us how to be servants for the Lord. He wanted us to be filled with the Holy Ghost so our souls wouldn't be lost. One day, when I was ten years old, he sat down with us and instructed us to "tarry" for the Holy Ghost. When we would hear people tarry in church, they would often start speaking in tongues. As a child I thought this meant they had received the Holy Spirit.

My grandfather anointed our heads with oil and told us to get down on our knees. Then he put his hands on our foreheads and started praying for our souls. We called on the name of Jesus constantly, or said, "Hallelujah," repeatedly. I remember feeling a strong sensation in my heart that gave me a warm, tingly feeling inside. I didn't speak in tongues, but I had felt the touch of the Holy Spirit! Tears came to my eyes. Even though I never discussed this with anyone in my family, from that day on I took church seriously. I learned to pray, and my grandfather would tell me to read the scriptures from the Bible out loud in church.

At this point my life consisted of school and church. Sundays were filled with church all day long, and we would have Bible study on Wednesday and Friday nights. We were in church so much; it became very boring when we didn't have any visitors. Sometimes the congregation was only our family, which consisted of four or five people. My brothers started doing things to avoid church, and even I sometimes wished I was watching TV instead. Rocky met some new girls, and Lionel got more involved with stealing. They fell away from the church, and they went "buck wild" in the streets. Lionel wanted to make money. So he signed up for a paper route delivering the *Macomb Daily News* after school, but that didn't last long. In between skipping school, stealing, and trying to make some money, he went astray. My grandparents started getting phone calls from the police about him. He was stealing big time from the malls, which led him to a police record.

School, at least, was cool. I could join different activities as long as I wasn't out at night by myself. I joined the school choir. My cousin, Velvet, and I also took over Lionel's paper route because he wasn't doing it right. The sales guy really wanted his papers delivered. So we started delivering the paper in the evenings after school. We had seventy-seven customers, and on the days we had to collect the money; some wouldn't answer the door. We would look through their window or peepholes and see shadows moving through the house to turn down the TV volume. To us this only meant we had to come back tomorrow and pray that they paid up. We delivered to all kinds of strange people.

My mother was always calling to check on us, still trying to exercise her rights. She would drive out to visit and insist that we go back with her. I wanted to see my mother, but I never wanted to visit her. All she did was smoke cigarettes, talk about a whole bunch of crazy nonsense, and get drunk. I remember crying one time because Lionel had taken off on one of his runs, and I had to go with her alone. She got very upset and started calling me names. I blocked her words out of my mind. The environment was so boring, and it certainly wasn't for kids. When it was time to take me back to my grandparents' house, I always praised God for hearing my prayers. I just didn't want to be with her anymore as she was depressing and even violent at times.

Jonathan lived in the rural part of town around twenty minutes from Mt. Clemens. We visited him on the weekends and sometimes during our school breaks. My brothers spent the majority of their weekends with him. I remember once, when we all went together to stay a few days, he offered us marijuana. My brothers accepted, but I refused to smoke because I was afraid. I started feeling very uncomfortable visiting him after this. Things began to change. I was going through puberty.

Jonathan, I always thought of him as my daddy was a big talker, and he would tell us stories about his life, sharing his wisdom and hoping to convert us. He'd talk for hours while we went for walks on the land and by the field. Sometimes we wouldn't get home till the sun went down. He took along his walking cane to use in case a snake or other critter crossed our path. I didn't talk much to him because I really didn't know what to say. Eventually he started talking about having custody of his children. He resented the fact that our mother had given us to his parents instead of him. I found out that she had never received child support from him, however. And she had threatened to turn him over to the police for not paying.

During our visits we could watch TV, sit around eating junk food, and stay up late. Daddy was easygoing, and we didn't have to worry about doing any chores. He finally persuaded me to ask my grandparents if I could visit him more often, and I agreed. As a child I was impressed knowing that I could actually sit around and enjoy cartoons and eat snacks whenever I wanted to. Whereas with my grandparents, I didn't have such luxuries. They were strict and believed in discipline; children should have chores and be involved in church. The more that I learned the difference between the two viewpoints, the more I started asking if I could visit Jonathan. But my grandparents weren't too thrilled about it. My Aunt Joyce would often come by and check on us when she was in the area. I noticed that when it was time for me to leave he would act possessive. It felt creepy.

One day when I was spending the night, I saw a spider crawling by my bed; and I asked my daddy to kill it. Later on that same night, he crawled into bed with me. I didn't know what to think or do; I clenched my muscles and lay there fearfully. When I got back to my grandparents' house, I didn't tell them about what my father was doing to us. I didn't want to take away his happiness when we would come to visit. I felt that we had a choice in the matter with the things that Jonathan was exposing to us. In between the visits, I overheard one of my aunts make comments to my grandmother about my visits at Jonathan's. They were saying that his mind is corrupted, and they questioned if it was safe for me to be over there. That's when I started paying attention to Jonathan's behavior. My aunt asked me if Jonathan had started reading the Bible to us. I replied, "no." Then she said that he had gotten deep into reading it alone for hours. He sat down with a few of his younger sisters, and he tried to convince them that it was okay to have sex with him. His belief came from the Bible in the First Testament book Genesis when God destroyed Sodom and Gomorrah. There were only a few survivors, Lot, and his daughters. During that time in order to multiply the earth, Lot had sex with his daughter. The chapter that talks about this story in the Bible signifies how and why this event happened. Looking back I realize he smoked a lot of weed then and talked about his beliefs and all kinds of weird stuff. He actually had a marijuana garden outside his house. As a little girl I couldn't see how someone smoking marijuana and reading the Bible could become distorted. This event opened my eyes to see how far from the truth Jonathan really was. He entered another door that illuminated light, but in reality it was only an illusion to deeper deception.

My father was the oldest son, and he didn't get along very well with his siblings with the exception of Aunt Joyce. I think it was because he was a rebel. He was the oldest boy, who had gone out into the world and adapted to a whole different way of living. Some of his ways weren't acceptable to his family; you could say he was like the prodigal son, the black sheep. My grandparents couldn't handle him or make him submit to God. My grandmother told me plenty of stories about Jonathan when he was a high roller out there in the world selling drugs. At one time he drove a hot red Mustang; he lived the fast life and ran around with many women. There was a rumor that my dad had fathered fifteen children in all, but I only met two of my half-sisters.

One day in a turn of events, Daddy experienced a very bad deal that almost cost him his life. It made him slow down. A guy who worked for Daddy, turned on him and put a pistol to his head. He was going to kill my father after robbing him. But Daddy prayed on the spot for God to spare his life! He promised God that he would quit dealing if he survived.

Thus, I was torn between my grandparents and parents. The fact that my parenting supervision came from both my grandparents and parents confused me. I didn't understand who to go to for answers to my questions or needs. I went to my granddaddy a lot because he was always kind and loving. However, his final word was always, "What did your madea say?" (Southern people use the term *madea*, short for "mother dear," when reverencing someone's mother.) This became very frustrating.

I remember having a toothache for months and complaining to my grandmother. Eventually she got tired of me crying, so they took me to the dentist. Whenever I got ill, my grandmother didn't believe in taking me to a doctor. I don't know if it was because she didn't believe in them or if it was a financial thing. She had a remedy for everything, however. For the most part it worked. I got ringworm on the back of my neck near my hairline, and she told me to put some black shoe polish on it three times a day. The itching went away gradually, and the ringworm dried up. She had also invented hair grease that she called "Lizard Grease," which grew my hair down my back. It stunk a little, but that stuff worked.

There was another adjustment in our diet. Now we were eating foods like black-eyed peas, greens, flapjacks (cornbread pancakes), okra, and white plate meat, a type of pork that's very salty and seasons greens very well. I missed cereal and milk, Hostess cakes, hamburgers, and casseroles. Those were the good old days when my stepfather Raymond took care of us. When I asked for food that I was used to eating, my grandmother felt I was being too picky. She would say there was plenty of food in her kitchen, but it was the kind you had to thaw out or cook from scratch. In addition, we always had a house full of family eating up the best food and messing up the house. When things in her house got messed up, broken, or came up missing, my grandmother accused me. She would yell at me to clean up everybody's mess after they left.

My grandmother had a lot of hostility and animosity towards my mother, and I could understand why. But this anger made my grandmother bitter, and she took it out on me.

I heard a lecture almost every day about how horrible my mother and brothers were. She didn't like us, and it showed. During these moments I would try to cling to my aunts and uncles, who were kind to me. I guess they felt sorry for me in a way because they would buy me popsicles and give me clothes from the Goodwill.

Eventually Lionel was sent to a youth home for stealing, and Rocky joined the army. Things changed drastically without Rocky and Lionel by my side. I got into a habit of praying when I got sick, or if I was having a bad day. I was in a place where I wasn't wanted, but I had nowhere else to go.

In the fall of 1978, I started school at George Washington Junior High. I was afraid to catch the school bus alone or to transfer between classes at school. It was a new world, and the time had arrived for me to start doing things independently. Fashion was a big thing, along with hairstyles and joining school activities. I needed lunch money everyday, but I had to go without many times. I wanted to dress nicely and fit in with my classmates, but I wasn't popular or good at anything that won me any special attention. I admired a couple of girls that I went to school with named Tina and Angela. They were both very popular, stylish, smart, and cute. I was always trying to fit in, but I didn't get accepted into the "in crowd." I fell in with the nerds and rejects. I was a loner a majority of the time, and I kept to myself.

Oftentimes I would fall asleep during class because I wasn't getting enough sleep at night. We had Bible study in the evenings on Wednesday and Friday nights, and sometimes revival ran for a week. I enjoyed drawing cartoon figures; however, my favorites were the Flintstones. My art class was my favorite period as I was able to be creative and make many of crafts. I discovered I was talented when it came to these kinds of hobbies.

My school offered dances, entertainment, and workshops on Fridays after school. I always wanted to go, but I was told that this was a part of Satan's work. I hardly complained or pouted if I didn't get my way because I always wanted to do what was pleasing to God. As time went on, I started to adjust to being in junior high and learning how to do things independently. But at the same time, my uncle Amos, who had Down's syndrome and attended a Special Ed school, was asked by his school to be in a movie. My grandparents believed that it was an attack from Satan. Uncle Amos was their youngest child; he was very likable and would dance, talk, and make friends with anyone. But because of this perceived threat, my grandparents decided to move down South to their second home in Alabama. They left town in a hurry with Amos, leaving me behind with Aunt Joyce. School was still in session at this time. I was fourteen when I received the news that I would be joining my grandparents down South, and it didn't set too well with me.

## ALABAMA – 1979

# CHAPTER 3

It was fall when I moved to Alabama, and the leaves were changing colors. I was escorted down South by cousin Red, who lived in Alabama. He told me stories about how beautiful the state was, and the air was fresher. Also, the food was seasoned better, and the people were hospitable. I didn't believe him because he was a talker.

We drove in my granddaddy's 1978 Regal Buick through many hills and next to high mountains. The ride was very long. As we got closer to the southern states, I started looking for the red dirt that he talked about. But I kept quiet because I felt confused about the change that was about to take place. We finally crossed the Alabama state line. As we drove through Birmingham, I thought, *Hey, this doesn't look bad*. But we kept driving through smaller and smaller towns, and we still hadn't made it to our destination! Eventually we turn onto Highway 219 South, which led us to Selma. I thought we were never going to stop driving.

We turned off of Highway 219 onto another road that led us to the red dirt. At the top of a long, steep hill, I saw plenty of red dirt that sat high off the bank of the road. There were trees everywhere, and the houses were far apart. All of a sudden the car stopped, and Red said, "Naima, you're home."

I panicked. "What did you say?"

"This is your grandparents' home," he said. "We're here."

"Are you for real?" I asked.

Then he blew the horn. Uncle Amos and my grandparents came out to greet us along with a bunch of dogs and cats. I looked around. There were no houses next door, no paved roads, or sidewalks. There were lots of trees, plenty of sky, and peaceful nature all around. Animal noises echoed in the air for miles. I couldn't express in words what I was feeling at this particular moment, but I was terrified. There were no kids in sight; I wanted to die. I couldn't believe that this was happening to me, and I had to live here until I turned eighteen.

It only got worse. I soon found out my grandparents' Alabama house was an old three-room with no bathroom. My granddaddy's daddy had built it in the late eighteen hundreds, so we had to use a pot called a slop jar for our toilet, the fireplace for our heat, and a wooden stove for cooking. I felt like I was living in *Little House on the Prairie*. We even had a well in the back of the house; this was our main source of water.

I started asking questions about why we had to move here, and why I had to move from my school. My new life down South was like opening up a novel on slavery during the late 1860s. I had seen *Roots*, and that gave me a pretty good idea of how hard life had been and still was for African Americans. Our way of living was not modern for the early eighties. I felt that this affected me emotionally as well as mentally.

School was in session, but my grandparents moved in slow motion when it came to handling affairs outside the home. In addition, there were other things we needed to attend to; we needed to get our living situation together. I was living with my grandparents and Uncle Amos in this little house. There was no privacy, and I had to do hard chores daily. I learned how to feed the animals, chop wood to make fires, and lock the animals up at night. I didn't have any idea how to successfully accomplish what I needed to do, and my grandmother didn't have a lot of patience in teaching me because I didn't seem content with my new life on Wakefield Hill. She fussed at me throughout.

This whole experience felt like a nightmare at a boot camp. My grandmother told me that I had no other choice but to go back North to live with my mother. She stressed how bad my life would be if I did that. That brought tears to my eyes; I had never imagined living like this, with no place else to go.

Finally my granddaddy enrolled me in school, and I started attending Suttles Junior High. My homeroom teacher's name was Ms. Hornbuckle. To my surprise, Uncle Amos was accepted to the same school, and he was in my homeroom.

I noticed that he could communicate very well with the kids in my classes. They seemed to be fond of him and did a lot of kidding around. I, however, felt ashamed of him because he wasn't normal looking and couldn't speak clearly. I was afraid that the kids would not like me because of his handicap, but that turned out to be untrue.

One day in our homeroom class before the bell rang, Amos was telling a classmate next to us about an incident that had happened the night before. I was giving him the mean look to be quiet, and of course he wouldn't listen. He told Mary Lynn that I had stolen his weenie off his plate. She laughed and wanted to know the whole story in detail. At that point, I stopped trying to hide the fact that we were related. I told her that he was my uncle. Mary Lynn explained how all the girls loved him to chase them around the school during recess. He made them laugh because he was a clown with a big heart. He would never hurt anyone, but he didn't take any mess from the kids at school. He'd warn you to quit messing with him. Some kids teased him just to provoke him, but if he came home complaining my grandmother didn't hesitate to handle it. The teachers respected him because my grandfather was a bishop; he was well known and respected by majority of the people he came into contact with. He had a beautiful spirit; and when he spoke, his voice drew your attention.

My third period teacher Ms. James called my name in class one day, and I responded, "What?"

She went off on me. "You are not up North, young lady. I don't know what they have been teaching you, but you better say '*yes ma'am*' and '*no sir*' to your elders down here."

My feelings were hurt, and I felt embarrassed. But after that episode, I began to catch on. My grandparents had never informed me of the different values and beliefs expected of me in the South, so I paid attention to how the other kids responded. My gym teacher Ms. Heibeger suggested that I try out for track. I joined the track team, but I didn't have any transportation. My grandmother didn't drive, and my grandfather was always away from home traveling. Nor did I have track teammates that lived close by. Things finally worked out for me to catch a ride from a staff worker at school who was related to one of my cousins.

Whenever I got the approval to go places, Uncle Amos wanted to follow. Eventually he joined the Special Ed track team, which turned out to be cool. He was popular, and he won the majority of his races. When we practiced at home, he'd run like a chicken with its head cut off; but I would always win. Once I got involved in track, things didn't seem so bad. I was learning how to be content. I met some kids that lived up the road—the Smiths and the Johnsons. My bus driver was Ms. Johnson; she was Cousin Red's mother. I didn't realize it, but the majority of people here were related to each other in some way or another.

Once track season ended, though, it got boring, and I wrote my father a letter explaining that I didn't like it down South. I asked him if he would come down to make things better for me. I explained about the transportation, how hard it was to go to town, and how I wanted to participate in some activities after school. Eventually, he did come down to live with us.

My father's way of keeping conversation was to talk about his life stories. I think he appreciated life to some degree because God had spared him and given him another chance. He also lived with us in this three-room house. We had a kitchen and a living room and one bedroom. My grandparents had made the living room into a bedroom, too, so I slept in the same room with my grandparents in my own big bed. The beds were made out of cast iron, and the mattresses were strong and solid.

One night my daddy took me and Amos for a ride to the store. We always wanted to go for a ride and get some junk food. The trip to the store was very long and dark. On our way back from the store, Daddy turned down a different road and pulled over, saying he had to check something out on the truck. He asked me to come to the back of the truck, but I said it was dark; and I was afraid. He insisted that I come see what he wanted, so I got out and walked around to the back where he was standing. He had pulled out his private. I became frightened and ran back to get inside the truck, and then I demanded that Amos sit in the middle between Daddy and me.

When we got home I didn't say anything about this to my grandparents because I knew that my relationship with my grandmother wasn't close. I saw they depended on my father for errands and chores around the place. I didn't know how to break the news.

On another occasion, my father asked me to come to his bedroom to look at some magazines. I didn't want to, but since he insisted; I went to see the magazines, which were X-rated. After he realized that I was walking away from him, he threw me on the bed and forced his lips to mine. He tried to put his tongue into my mouth, but I struggled up from the bed and told him "no." Then I ran to the kitchen where my grandmother was. I don't know if she could see the expression on my face, but I was confused and in a state of disbelief.

This was the episode that caused me to withdraw and put some distance between my father and me because he was becoming very obsessive. He made me wash his feet one night, and he told me to read the Bible to him. I had read a scripture about how disobedient children would not live out their days: "Honor your father and your mother, as the Lord your God has commanded you, that your days may be long, and that it may be well with you in the land which the Lord your God is giving you" (Deuteronomy 5:16). I was too afraid to tell on my father for fear of the outcome. I started clinging more to my grandfather to protect me. I think my grandparents saw that my contact with him had changed. They never questioned my behavior, but in my heart I think they knew something wasn't right.

On Friday nights my father would go around the curve to Bennie Mae's house and drink liquor. Some folks said she was mixing it with rubbing alcohol. When he got home, he would wake everybody up, talking loudly, saying stupid stuff, and ready to fight anybody that got in his way. He carried a rifle, and he had a very unruly temper when he got drunk. This eventually caused my grandfather to ask him to leave. My father got very upset, but my grandfather took a stand. And once my father moved out, things were a lot better. He built a house across the way on the family land. His drinking persisted, and over time it got worse. From that point on, he became a living nightmare. I would do anything to avoid seeing him.

Whenever I was at school, I was always daydreaming about being free. My eighth grade graduation was coming up, and I was counting down the days and years to go. I had a cousin I really admired named Joy; she was beautiful, and we were the same age. She lived in Detroit, and she kept me up-to-date on all the latest fashions, dances, hairstyles, and slang. My grandmother asked Joy's mother, my Aunt Barbara, to send me a white dress to wear for my graduation. Aunt Barbara dressed her kids with the finest clothes because they were privileged.

The day that box came I was so excited to see my dress. I opened it quickly, but when I touched the dress to hold it up; I became angry. The material was very thick. It was late spring in Alabama, and the temperature was in the eighties on most days. I knew that I was going to look stupid and feel uncomfortable wearing that dress, but I had no choice. I forced myself to like it by tying a silk ribbon around the waist. That brought out more style. I knew that the dress had come from the Goodwill, but what bothered me the most was that Aunt Barbara didn't care that it was out of season.

Aunt Barbara and her kids came, along with more cousins and my sister, to visit that summer. It was very nice to have company, but they could never get too comfortable at grandmother's house. It was very old and "way too small" to hold all of the family. Some of the menfolk slept over at my father's house. But it didn't bother me that we didn't have enough sleeping room as long as I was happy. I was enjoying my cousins down to the very last moment before saying good-bye because I wasn't used to being isolated. They all shared my pain. I remember crying because I wanted to go back with them. My grandfather comforted me, saying I could ride with him up North when he took his trip. Once they all left, life was boring and lonely again, especially when I was out of school for the summer.

My grandfather decided to start farming, so he bought twenty-five acres of land. He figured that this would be how he would feed his family when they came down in the summers to visit. The farming began. And before I knew it, I was in a field putting seeds in the ground and walking down many rows. I was angry because it was hot and sunny. I saw no end to this madness, nor did I see why it was necessary. My grandmother told me that I could stay home if I wanted to, but I knew the consequences. I would have to deal with my father's harassment. I saw no way out. We had a lot of seeds to plant, so my grandfather asked the Smith family to help us because they had eight strong children. He paid the hired help, but my wages were in the form of a pop and a honey bun. Trust me, it was refreshing to have a cold soda and a honey bun. After working from sunup till noon, it was something to look forward to.

During the first few weeks of this, I wanted to run away. Never in my wildest dreams would I have fathomed that I would be working in a field one day. It had never occurred to me that my life would follow the journey of *Roots*! I couldn't figure out why we had to do this hard labor; it wasn't like we ate a lot. Granddaddy's idea did make money, and it fed the family. But the labor, time, and profits never balanced out with what he invested.

Once the crops were ready, we packed up everything that needed to go North. My father was the driver, and granddaddy conducted the funds, transportation, and food for the trip. He was a man of integrity and a well-respected human being with many visions and dreams. I listened to him faithfully because he had the anointing of God over his life. He was a praying man, and I wanted to please him by being smart so he could reward me. He was fair and wise and always had something kind to say; he never doubted you, unless you showed him otherwise.

We loaded the truck with watermelons, greens, okra, sweet potatoes, cucumbers, tomatoes—you name it. We had it. While up North, we sold all the produce. And I visited with my cousins who I had missed dearly. We stayed for almost two weeks, and then we headed back South.

I coordinated my new clothes and hand-me-downs. I was starting high school at East Perry High, located in the rural part of Selma off a main highway that led to many towns like Marion, Selma, and Centreville. I wore my hair in either two twists or two French braids. I was quiet in school and very shy. I stayed low key because I didn't want to attract any attention. Uncle Amos attended the Special Education classes at East Perry. We were split up in high school with a different homeroom, but the school system moved him along each year according to my grade level.

As a freshman I didn't participate in any after-school activities because my father had to approve and be a part of everything. I lost trust in him, and I realized that he wasn't the nice father I thought he was. Inside my mind I felt trapped because I saw no way out. I didn't know who to trust with all these emotions that were rolling around inside my heart. Therefore, I suppressed them as though they didn't exist. But at high school, I felt more independence because it was a bigger school. I did frequent daydreaming during my classes, fantasizing about being in California where my favorite cousin lived. I continued to feel that my life resembled Kunta Kinte's in *Roots* because my mind was always fixated on leaving Alabama. I knew that I couldn't share how I felt with anyone down South; I believed that my opinion would rub off in a bad way. I tried to understand how people were content living in the rural areas where it was boring and slow.

During my lonely times at home, I would read the Bible and inspirational literature and write letters to Jesus. I would tell Him all about my fears and troubles. I thanked Him for the times when I didn't have to submit to the negativity of my father, who was acting like the devil and being a hindrance in my life. I realized that he wasn't going anywhere else to live because he had no dreams. Since I couldn't avoid seeing him, I distanced myself emotionally and mentally.

Eventually I fell into the routine of going to school, church, doing chores, and helping our elderly cousins who lived across the road. My grandfather had cousins called Cutten Pete and Cutten Louise, who were husband and wife. Cutten Pete would often ask if I could come and sit with Cutten Louise. She had diabetes, and both her legs had been amputated. She was nice and kept a clean house, and I got paid for sitting with her; and I got to eat snacks. Sometimes I was able to miss out on going to the field and doing chores.

One evening while I was sitting with Cutten Louise, she rolled her wheelchair to the back of the house. Cutten Pete was preparing to take his nightly walk, and as he was walking past me for the door he grabbed one of my breasts and smiled. I was terrified, and I jerked my body away. After that incident, I tried to avoid going over there. I didn't tell my grandparents about this because I didn't want to stir up any trouble.

My cousin Velvet came down to attend school. This was an adventure because she and I didn't get along. She was starting the fifth grade at Suttles Elementary, and I had to show her the ropes regarding chores and farming. We argued a lot, and sometimes she wanted to fight me when she couldn't have her way.

My grandmother showed favoritism towards Velvet because she was cute and very dark-skinned. She had been teased about her skin complexion constantly while growing up, which caused her to have low self-esteem. We had many fair and light- skinned cousins. And I think because Velvet had been teased about her complexion, it scarred her. She was a troublemaker and tattletale. Whenever she and I would disagree, I got punished, which caused me to dislike her. She would start the devilment, but when I called her names; she would run and tattle about anything as small as a word or a dirty look. I tried to get along with her. She eased some of my burdens and filled that lonely space.

One evening after tending to the chores, feeding the animals, and locking up the chicken coop, we realized we had forgotten to bring a bucket of water into the house. It was nighttime, and we didn't have a drop of water in case of an emergency. We had to go outside to draw water out of the well. It was pitch dark, and we both were pulling the bucket from the bottom of the well. Velvet heard something in the bushes near the woods, and she let go of the rope, which caused me to lose my grip. I knew that if we allowed the rope to hit the bottom, we would get a beating. So I struggled to hold onto it, and by the time I got a good grip; it had scorched the insides of my hands. I had severe rope burns on my fingers and hands. I cried because of the pain, and I couldn't write in class for at least a week.

My father visited from time to time. I believe he had a plan up his sleeve to wean me back into his sickness. On my fifteenth birthday, he bought me a cake, and I received a few cards from some friends at school. When I got home from school, Velvet and Uncle Amos were eager to go over to Jonathan's to eat some ice cream and cake. I went along figuring I was safe in case my father tried anything because Velvet was there. She and Uncle Amos could talk to him openly about anything. Although I was apprehensive about being there, I remained quiet to observe the environment. Daddy took some photos of us, and he asked if he could take some pictures of us in the woods. We never agreed to do anything like that, but as you can see his mind wasn't right.

Since we didn't go along with his plan, he started harassing us. He would come to my grandparents' house when he was intoxicated, telling them that Velvet and I were out at night riding on a motorcycle and running with boys. My grandfather didn't buy this because he knew where we were at nighttime. Next, Daddy took us to town one Saturday. There he bought us some groceries, and he gave each of us money to buy some personal things. But after we got back from town, we discovered that his stuff had gotten mixed in with ours. We walked over to his house to give him his food and to thank him again. When we got up to leave, my father told me that I couldn't go. He told Velvet to run on home. She didn't like his answer or the expression on my face, so she ran home to tell my grandmother what was happening.

My father held me hostage at his house, threatening to shoot me if I tried to leave. He explained that he would kill me, and that I was full of shit. He went on about blowing my brains out if I kept fucking with him. He talked about all kinds of mess, accusing me of liking my uncles, and asking which boy was I letting feel on me. I endured this verbal, mental, and emotional abuse for approximately eight hours, all the time praying to the Lord to hear my cry. I didn't believe that anyone was ever going to rescue me. Eventually, my grandmother came over and called to my father, but he wouldn't answer the front door. Then she walked around to the side door of his house, which he left open. She asked him why he was keeping me there. He told her to mind her own business, but she paid him no attention. She told him the law was going to get him if he didn't let me go. She demanded that he let me leave. I immediately ran out the door all the way home. I will never forget that day. I can't recall ever going to his house willingly or alone after that episode. He'd traumatized me to the point that I would get tense whenever I heard his voice or if someone said his name. When he came over to visit my grandparents, I would go inside the house and act busy.

When the fall settled in again, we were able to rest from laboring in the fields. By the time spring came, Velvet was getting homesick and started complaining to her mother. Her mother drove down to pick her up, and my life went back to the same old routine. I was never content being isolated, especially when school was out. I felt that there wasn't anything worthwhile to wake up for. There was no place to go but to the field. At least on Sundays, we would go to church and sometimes to town. The most exciting part about going to town was eating at the restaurants.

We heard that the local church was giving out free lunches during the week at noontime. This was a state-funded program that lasted a month. Uncle Amos and I were able to get only a few lunches, but it was cool, regardless. We got the chance to see some different faces besides the animals' and each others'. Nothing was more exciting to me than imagining the day when I would graduate from high school and leave Alabama. Those days were marked on a secret calendar in my heart.

I remained humble throughout my circumstances because I had to trust God. I always believed what the scripture said about disobedient children not living out their days, in spite of the brutality inflicted by my father. I wanted God to bless me to see a better life, despite the fact that whenever my grandmother got upset with me, she declared that I was going to turn out like my mother, abused and mistreated by men, violent, unruly, homeless, boastful, and rotten to the core. I wouldn't accept her words; instead, I fought hard to be a better person. I prayed to Jesus in silence to help me survive this life.

One day, one of my aunts called my grandmother to give her some disturbing news about my mother. She had murdered her newest husband Leroy, and she had been incarcerated. This was another hard tragedy to face. When I spoke to Rocky about it, his version of what had happened was that our mother and Leroy were drinking and arguing. Rocky told them to separate that evening because he could tell somebody was going to get hurt. Shortly after he left, the neighbors heard gunshots coming from the house, and they reported it to the police. The police marched in to find Leroy lying in a pool of blood. He was pronounced dead on the scene.

Months later my mother was released after pleading insanity. She was clinically ill, and society released her without any provisions regarding her behavior. It was harvest time in Alabama, and the crops were ready to be taken North again. I pleaded to go on this trip, but my father had another agenda. He tried to get me to ask my grandparents if I could live with him. He continued to plot and scheme against my innocence. His plan while we were in Mt. Clemens this time was to go to the courthouse to file for custody. He picked a fight because I wouldn't agree. I told him that I didn't want to live with him, and as I turned away he hit me in the head with his fist. I lost my balance and went tumbling down forty-two stairs. Once I got up, I started crying and cussing at him; and I took off running outside. Aunt Joyce came to see what was happening, and she asked him why he had hit me. I have no idea what his reply was.

The spirit of fear grew inside my heart as I imagined him killing me. He was tormenting me in every way he could to gain control! When my cousins visited, they could see and feel my pain. They would say words of encouragement to help me, such as: "you'll be eighteen soon," and "you don't have much longer." Nothing seemed to comfort me; I truly wanted to die. No one knew about the agony going on inside my mind, or my thoughts of suicide.

My cousins finally asked my grandparents and father why I couldn't live in Michigan with them. My grandparents wanted to let me go. They knew it was my desire to leave, but father harassed them about it and put fear in them. My aunt in California also wanted to take me in and send me to school, but my father wasn't having it! I already knew that he wasn't going to go for that because he wanted to ruin me. I got on my knees and prayed to Jesus, my only source of hope. I needed this Jesus that my granddaddy preached about more than ever. I believed that one day I would be set free if I could be patient and do well. I cried for many days and nights; my spirit was broken. I was angry, and the agony was piercing my mind.

All of this made my grandmother more distanced around me; she could see that I was very unhappy. It was the end of the summer, and I was getting excited about starting school and dying to get away from Wakefield Hill. I had to bounce back to reality and accept my situation. I started preparing for school by looking through magazines like *Right On* and *Ebony*. I wanted to go back to school looking different for my sophomore year. I wanted a fresh new look. I wore my hair down, and I put on lipgloss. And for the first time in my life, I got a lot of attention. I kind of liked the attention, to tell you the truth. I had a few classes mixed with the seniors and juniors, and they'd flirt with me and tell me that they liked the new look.

In my home economics class I met a new girl from Chicago. Twila was outgoing, pretty, petite, and smart—but very mouthy. She had that "Chi-Town flair"; she wore very stylish clothes, and her hair was pretty. Most of all, we clicked because we were from up North. We became friends just through that connection.

It was common down South to start courting at the age of fifteen. And if you weren't dating, you would be teased. I hid the fact that I enjoyed the attention of being flirted with. I was too scared to let anyone know that I couldn't date or get out of the house. One day in home economics, we had to form groups to start doing different projects. A boy name Saul Melton, who was a senior, joined my group. He was flirting with me, and he offered to buy my portion of supplies. Saul and I became friends. He started calling me "little girl" when he'd see me in between changing classes. That didn't bother me; he was the oldest, and that was his way of saying he liked me.

Soon Saul asked if I would be his girlfriend. I told him that I couldn't have a boyfriend, so he asked if I would be his girlfriend at school. I was afraid of having a boyfriend, but I liked the attention. So I secretly became his girlfriend with no idea how I was going to pull this off. Saul asked me to go with him into our algebra teacher's room. Then he pulled me close to him, and he put his lips to mine. It all happened quite fast in between changing classes. I immediately ran out of the room to make it to my next class before the bell rang. When he kissed me, I had my glasses on. But I remember seeing stars. I felt so dorky and ashamed. I didn't know what the devil I had been thinking because I had never kissed a boy.

Saul asked me if I would be his prom date, and if I could have company. I knew that the pressure was going to start. I had dreaded this moment, and I found myself feeling even dumber. I told him that my grandparents were strict, and I wasn't old enough to court. But he kept asking me, trying to find ways to convince me that he could make it happen. I couldn't lie to my grandparents, and I didn't dare let my father know about us.

Saul finally chilled out since he could detect my nervousness. He was popular in school, and he was known for talking, singing in the talent shows, and goofing off. He never seemed to care about doing his lessons, and he would ask different girls to write his papers and do his homework. One thing he seemed to do well was type. I was impressed because I didn't know how to type.

The seniors were preparing for graduation, and that meant that Saul would be leaving East Perry. I was able to attend his graduation because some of the folks that lived on my side of town were seniors, too. So my grandparents allowed me to catch a ride. It was like winning the lotto when I got out the house to attend anything after school without my family. This time of year was never pleasant because I knew what my summer entailed. I can truly say that, despite my cousins visiting, I hated my summers more than my school life in the South. I counted the days down to the hours to when I would graduate. I knew this meant a lot to my grandparents. They said that once I turned eighteen and graduated from high school, they were done. That stayed in the back of my mind, but whenever my father heard it he'd say something different. To him I wasn't grown until I turned twenty-one. I blocked that out of my mind along with anything else he had to say, because I knew that he was going to rain on my parade.

Listening to my classmates discussing summer plans to go away and visit family, I felt lonely on the inside because I didn't have anyone in whom I could confide. I had to live with my circumstances until my change came.

One summer day when we went to the field to work the crops, it got so hot that I just didn't have the will to work. My grandmother started fussing because she didn't believe in me sitting around or lounging under a shade tree. She believed in working like a slave. When I looked up, I saw my granddaddy heading towards me. He was walking very fast and slinging his arms back and forth behind his back while he whistled. To see his arms moving in haste that meant that he was serious. At this point I got scared; I knew that either I was going to get a whipping or be punished in some way. My grandfather told me to get in the truck and drive. I didn't quite understand what he meant, but I immediately climbed inside the truck. Then I put it into gear, and I push down on the gas to accelerate the truck. He told me to watch for the potholes and to stay on the road. The branches were hitting the sides of the truck because the road was so narrow.

From that day on my grandfather put me behind the steering wheel to drive him all over Alabama. I was so happy; this gave me a chance to meet people and see different towns and cities. We would rise early and have breakfast before we left for church on Sundays. Driving for my granddaddy relieved me of feeding the animals, drawing water out of the well, and chopping wood. By the time we got home, it would be pitch dark and bedtime. I didn't have my driver's license, but I drove carefully. We went to Marion, Selma, Mobile, Uniontown, Centreville, and other towns I had never heard of before. We made our summer trip to Michigan, sold our produce, and got back on the highway for home. This time for some reason I didn't feel sad when it came time to leave Michigan. I had started looking at my life differently because I was sixteen years old. I felt that I could endure my last two years.

When school started, I was sad that Saul wasn't there. In many ways I was missing him, and I wondered what he was doing. I was always thinking about turning eighteen and being on my own. I imagined my whole world changing. I took driver's education, and I felt pretty confident about it. Months went by, and one day while I was in school a classmate told me that Saul was visiting. I thought he had forgotten all about me. I got the butterflies and panicked as he stopped me during my class break. We hugged, and then he asked me to go with him to an empty classroom. I told him that I had to go to my next class, but he said that he had covered for me. Before I knew it, he had me pinned up in the back corner of the classroom. One minute we were talking, and then he was kissing all over my lips. Time zoomed by pretty fast; before I knew it I had skipped my fourth and fifth period classes. I knew then that I had to leave him, and we said our good-byes.

My conscience had been trying to tell me that it was too risky to skip two classes, but I wasn't paying it any mind. After being reprimanded, I felt stupid for getting suspended from school for a week. I told my grandparents the truth; I had skipped class to talk to Saul. My grandfather wanted to know if we had had sex, and I told him that we had only talked. I only prayed my father wouldn't find out. I avoided seeing him, although my suspension was all the talk through the family in Michigan and California. It felt like my world had ended. It was the longest week in my life. Plus, I couldn't talk to Saul to tell him that he had lied to me about covering me for skipping class. And he couldn't call me because I had never given him my number.

When I returned to school, the students stared at me because the rumor had spread all over. I heard that Saul had gone back to Chicago, and I was relieved because he had put so much pressure on me. But he started secretly sending me love letters, pictures, cards, and money. I couldn't wait to open the mailbox and see a letter addressed from him. It would make my whole week. I didn't know what to say back to him, but when I wrote to give him my phone number; the words just came. Eventually these letters started to take effect; my heart starting feeling things that I had never felt before. I couldn't keep my mind off Saul; the more I thought of him, the deeper my feelings grew. My unhappiness at home seemed to subside because there was something else going on inside my little heart.



As time went on, I never thought about where this fairy tale was heading. Saul had plenty of opportunities where he was living to date and find another woman to settle down with. But he kept calling regardless of the fact that I couldn't go on a date with him. As spring of 1983 rolled around, Saul called to invite me to his family reunion during the Fourth of July. I wanted to go badly because I really felt that I loved him. I rehearsed how I would ask for permission. I was very excited, but I also was afraid that my father would object.

The day finally came when I got up the nerve to ask my grandmother. She asked me a lot of questions, but Saul had it all planned out. He had invited my grandmother to come with us as a chaperone. Saul came to pick us up, and my grandmother also decided to bring Uncle Amos. After we got to the reunion, I started feeling all special and grown. I met the whole family, and I learned that Saul was the baby of fourteen children, though some were deceased. There were sixty grandchildren and counting. It was cool to see people that I had gone to school with, and they were shocked to see me. Saul persuaded me to ride to town, but I wasn't sure if that was being smart. He asked different people to cover for him by keeping my grandmother and uncle occupied. When we made it to town, he made sure that anybody and everybody saw us together. He wanted to make a statement that I was his girlfriend to feed his ego.

After we got back from town, the look on my grandmother's face said trouble. She felt that there was going to be real trouble on her end if I was pregnant. I promised her that I hadn't had sex with Saul; he had tried to go there, but I lied and said that I was on my flower. And it was the truth; I was too scared to have sex.

When school started, I had this burst of energy. I was finally a senior, and my time was coming. I was eager to do my chores and whatever my grandparents wanted. I could see that my life was about to change in a matter of months. I enjoyed being a senior because I received a lot of attention. Saul promised to give me money if I made good grades. So for the first time in my life, I got on the ball. In all my twelve years of schooling, this was the best report card that I had ever received. Saul gave me five dollars for every "B," and the money increased for every "A." I applied myself and got focused in school. I prayed and kept a journal of my letters to Jesus. I listened and paid attention to everything that I came in contact with. I wore makeup often and jazzed up my clothes. I didn't let anything get me down to the point that I couldn't deal with it. I let things roll off my shoulders like they never happened.

My classmates were talking about going away to different colleges and universities. I had never had any educational dreams; I only wanted to get away from my father. I realized later on in my life that because of him, I wasn't able to live to be who I wanted to be. I was forced to become this frightened little girl who struggled for acceptance, love, and protection. I couldn't enjoy my youth like my peers; I was too busy trying to protect my spirit, body, and soul from the evils that tried to destroy me. I prayed to King Jesus, thanking Him for protecting me to live to see some accomplishments that I thought I had never see.

During the week of my eighteenth birthday I received a package from my mother. Inside the box there was a birthday card, some money and my birth certificate. Jonathan is listed as the father. I felt confused about why my mother lied to me years ago by saying that another man was my father. I wanted to ask her about it, but I was too afraid to upset her. She had an unruly temper and a streak of violence. I concluded that it was meaningless to confront her, because both of my parents were "mentally and emotionally unhealthy."

Finally graduation was approaching, and my classmates were planning the prom. I still had issues with my father controlling my participation with my senior outings. He expected me to ask him for permission first. I didn't want to go to prom because I didn't have anything nice to wear. Plus Saul wasn't home. During this time I finally opened up to Ms. King, my home economics teacher, about my father's abuse. She started crying. She had taught us about these matters during the years she was my teacher, so I don't know what made me confess about it at this late stage. But she offered to help me and wanted to know my plans after graduation. I told her that I was leaving as soon as I graduated, and I assured her that I would be all right because I knew that I would do the two things that were required of me: graduate from high school and turn eighteen.

On graduation night my classmates arranged a party in Selma. My father didn't want me to go. I was standing outside his car in the school's parking lot, debating and negotiating. One of my closest classmates interrupted, asking what I was going to do. I agreed to walk off with her. Rocky was in town for a few weeks to help Jonathan out with some construction and upkeep on the property. Whenever Rocky's life was bad, he would show up and disappear when things cool down. When I returned home after the party, I could hear Jonathan talking about me to Rocky. I felt that I had a choice for the first time in my life, and I'm still glad that I took that stand.

At this point my grandmother didn't care anymore about what I did. She wanted me to be on my own because she was tired of watching over me. She felt that she had given me all she could, and that it was a burden to protect me. I had my things packed days before graduation. My grandfather's cousin that lived in Birmingham, who came down to visit other kinfolks and attend church on Sundays, agreed to take me to Birmingham to catch the Greyhound bus. I had no idea how much my bus fare would cost, but all I needed was a one-way ticket going to Detroit. I was blessed to have enough money from my graduation gifts. Ms. King really blessed me by giving me some extra money for food on my journey.

During this particular time, my father had left to take his girlfriend, Ms. Patty, to Florida. I knew that if I didn't make my move while he was away, it would be terrifying to escape once he returned. He wanted me to stay in Alabama and attend college at a local junior college. He even offered to let me drive his car. But I wasn't listening to anything that he had to say that would delay me any longer.

When Cousin Finest arrived to pick me up, I couldn't believe that the day had finally come. I put my bags in the trunk of his car and gave my grandparents and Uncle Amos bear hugs. I expressed to them that I was thankful, and I felt that they were glad for me. But I detected sadness, too. They told me to be careful and to remember the stories they had taught me about calling on the name of Jesus. As we drove away from Wakefield Hill, I looked up at the bank and stared at the red dirt. I thought that I was leaving for good.

Perry County was the place where my life was shaped by the many days that I spent in the fields farming, driving my granddaddy to church, singing those spiritual Southern hymns, learning morals, and praying to Jesus, who protected me from all of the hurt and harm that came my way. I'll always remember my roots, the struggles, and all the pain. Thoughts were bouncing all around inside my head as Cousin Finest put me on the bus. I sat in the front; and when the bus drove off, I waved at him.

## MICHIGAN – 1984

# CHAPTER 4

I traveled through the night, and I had a layover in Tennessee. I was not in a hurry to get to Michigan because I was enjoying the long bus ride. I had napped off, and as soon as I opened my eyes, I could see rivers. The sunlight shone brightly. We crossed over the Kentucky Bridge. I tried to turn my head around to look behind me, but there wasn't enough view, so I imagined the many miles that I had traveled. I smiled in disbelief that this couldn't be just a dream. I came to my senses while listening to the bus's engine. The bus driver kept trying to talk to me about life and wanted to know where I was going. But I had been warned to be careful and to not say much.

During my layover, I called Saul collect. He was excited to hear my voice; then he asked me to come to Chicago, but of course I couldn't. I gave him contact information for my family in Michigan. My aunt Christine was expecting my arrival at the bus station downtown. She wasn't able to pick me up, but she had made arrangements for a friend of the family to be there.

At this point I didn't know what my life was going to be like or where I was headed. However, I kept an optimistic attitude and promised myself that

I wouldn't change to become the ugly things that my grandmother had spoken into my life. I had no realistic goals. When I was fifteen, I had dreamed about going off to Hollywood to become an actress until my father lectured me about how I could turn out ruined by drugs and alcohol—or end up committing suicide. I had also seen an ad in *Ebony* magazine about being paid for writing songs or poems. I was intrigued, but my father was discouraging about this as well.

After living in Detroit with Aunt Christine and Velvet for a short time, I felt that I needed to move on. I wasn't in school or doing anything with my time except watching Velvet. I started bouncing from one aunt's house to the next. Finally I became so bored that I decided to go visit Saul in Chicago. He sent me the money to take the bus.

I had heard so much about Chicago, and I had always wanted to see it. But I was disappointed by the amount of litter and people hanging out at all times of night. I had never seen so many young, pregnant, teenage girls standing at the bus stops. I was shocked and sad to see things like this in a place that had sounded like a city of opportunities. I learned quickly that every big city has its poverty, ghetto, and crime.

During this trip I also visited my dear friend Twila. She had a different spirit from the girl that I had met in Alabama. She talked about gangs, and her whole demeanor was aggressive. I thought she had an easy life, and things were given to her because she was beautiful. When she expressed that she didn't think that Saul was right for me, I was shocked; but I didn't follow her advice. She treated Saul badly, though, because she knew that he was a slickster and believed he was not good for me. But I was deeply in love with him, and I couldn't see what this meant for my future. I didn't care who said what; I was crazy about him. He was handsome and a skilled welder, and his kindness drew people to him. He was generous and fun, a big Southern talker.



Still, I was seeing things about him that I hadn't imagined when I was in high school. Whenever we went places, women were flirting with him in my face. It made me behave violently, and I started using cuss words a lot. I stayed only for a weekend, and I left unhappy—but still in love. And I gave him something that was precious to my soul: my virginity. It wasn't romantic like I had imagined it would be. Maybe it was because I wasn't ready to be a woman. But I felt that I loved him, and I wanted to make a life with him. I went back to Michigan feeling down and trying to figure things out. I was trying to find stability.

Aunt Vanessa is Jonathan's baby sister, and we are six years apart in age. She called to ask if I wanted to live with her and work at her place of employment. I accepted her offer, and by the end of the summer, I was employed working at a bacon factory in Mt. Clemens. It was cool at first because I was earning a paycheck, but I didn't like the heat or the second shift. I also had a hard time trying to get a stable place to live; my family's homes had limited space, and they had enough kids already. It was tough trying to live out of a bag and a suitcase. I became committed to the job, however. I started hanging out at the bars with my aunt and her friends. I met guys there that wanted to date me, but I didn't find any prospects interesting.

One attractive guy from Detroit, who looked like Prince, asked me out. He was fine, but I wasn't feeling the dating scene. I continued working hard and saving my money. I bought a few clothes and babysat for my family. Saul called occasionally towards the end of the summer. He made promises, and then he broke them. I felt that I loved him, but I didn't know why. Still, he was the only man I had eyes for. I just didn't know how to move on. I started losing hope about being with him in terms of marriage and having kids. I started to feel a sense of loss. How could this be when I was free and eighteen? I didn't understand what the world had to offer. I was hung up on being in love and feeling loved.

Eventually I got tired of waiting for Saul to come visit. As the seasons changed, fall was approaching. And I started to forget all about Chicago and Saul. Then, during Christmas, I got a surprise visit from him. I felt so happy and special; the fairy tale was back! It was snowing outside, and the tree limbs were frozen. Christmas music was playing everywhere I went, and everybody seemed to be in the holiday spirit. I wanted time to stand still forever because I was feeling love. I was finally getting some one-on-one attention, and my heart was feeling things that I wanted to feel.

Saul had to leave to get back to work in Chicago, and saying good-bye was hard. As the months went by, we kept in touch and sent cards and letters. In spring of 1985 Saul was laid off his job, and he decided to visit to see if he wanted to relocate. We stayed in a small kitchenette, because shackin' wasn't permitted in my upbringing. My grandparents believed in marrying you off by age sixteen. But I was happy that we were together, and not having to rush our time. We had, in the past, talked about having a family and where we would like to live.

One day Saul received a call from his brother letting him know that a trucking company wanted to offer him a job back in Chicago driving trucks. He was also being called back to his former employer after being laid off. I panicked about the news, and then we found out that I was pregnant. Saul kept saying that I had better not be; but I was, and that was the truth. He was in a dilemma over choosing to drive trucks or accept going back to his old job and be a father. This, of course, changed the direction of both our lives. I pleaded for us to stay together as a family. Saul declined the truck driver's job, and he decided to go back to work in Chicago. We spent a month apart while he worked on a plan to move me there. He called to let me know that everything was set up and when to expect his bus arrival. I packed everything I had in my car. I rode downtown to the bus station in Detroit to pick him up, and this was the evening that I eloped to Chicago.

Illinois – 1985

# CHAPTER 5

Saul had a one-bedroom apartment waiting for us on the South Side. I wasn't happy about being pregnant, but I knew that I loved this man enough to have his baby. Saul had been good to me, and he had made a lot of promises that I was expecting him to fulfill. All I could see now was that I needed to be with him because I never wanted to be abandoned with a baby.

It was difficult to find work during my pregnancy. Saul worked as a welder at a parts and services company, and his income was decent considering his age. He was fortunate to receive the position through one of his brothers, who had been a supervisor there. He informed me that there would be times when his job would lay him off, however.

Shortly after settling into our new apartment, I called back home to Michigan to let Aunt Vanessa know that I had made it safely. It turned out that my mother was out on a manhunt looking all over for me. She had even put in a missing person's police report. Aunt Vanessa was the only one who knew what I was planning to do, and she also was the only one that I had confided in about my pregnancy. She said my mother had paid her a visit, and she demanded that she tell her where

I was hiding. Vanessa told her that I had decided to move to Chicago, and that was all she knew. My mother had no way of verifying this with me.

Saul wanted me to contact my family, so they wouldn't be worried. The news that Aunt Vanessa gave me, however, was that my mother had plans for me to support her financially. She was hoping that we could live together, but that was out of the question now. I was relieved that I had moved out of state. I knew I couldn't trust her behavior. I had never planned on being a part of her misery. Our bond was broken.

I finally ended up calling her from a payphone two weeks after I got settled, so she would leave Aunt Vanessa alone. She was talking fast and cussing at me, asking lots of questions about "who is this Saul guy?" I briefly told her that I was in love with him, and I explained how we met in high school. Then I said I wanted her to cool it with looking all over for me. I promised to write her and tell her more details. I know my mother was not happy with my decisions, but I had to be direct with her. I hoped that my frankness would calm her down a bit. She felt that I was hiding something from her, and she threatened to get Saul if things weren't right when she saw him.

During this time, I was content, but a part of me was scared. I had no mother figure around to tell me the things that I needed to know about having a baby. During my pregnancy, my eyes were opened; I could see the effects that it had on my relationship with Saul. It slowed things down; I was getting tired as my body grew into the pregnancy. We weren't able to drive around at all times of night to sightsee, take long walks, eat out at the restaurant, or shop at the mall. And additionally, new bills were coming in.

The first layoff experience with Saul occurred five months after I relocated to Chicago. It was the beginning of hard times and struggles. The job that he held was a supply and demand business. He could be laid off every four months; it was the risk that he took when he decided to go back to work for this employer. At this particular time while I was pregnant, Saul was denied unemployment benefits due to overdrawing from his last layoff. So there was no money coming in. That hurt us, but with Saul's diverse skills and his big brother's help, he was back working in no time. I wanted to contribute, but I was getting further along in my pregnancy. I know that this was definitely hard on Saul. He suggested that I could have had an abortion when we were back in Michigan, and I was very hurt thinking that he wanted to run.

Saul started smoking more marijuana and drinking, saying that it helped him to relax and relieve a lot of stress. It didn't bother me because I felt as long as he was treating me the same, I couldn't complain. Then he started hanging out on the weekends saying he was at his brother's house on the South Side.

Autumn was settling upon us when I decided to write my mother so she could stop worrying about me. One evening while I was alone at home, my doorbell rang; and I answered it. It was my mother, out of the blue. I didn't know how she was going to react because she had never met Saul. But during her visit, we became friends for the first time. She wanted to see what kind of living conditions I was in and meet Saul face to face. She also introduced me to her mother's half-sister's family, who actually lived five minutes away in "The Chicago Housing Projects", Altgeld Gardens. When I met them, they embraced me with kindness. However, I didn't feel too comfortable with one particular cousin. I didn't receive positive vibes from her. Her aura was like a scarlet letter releasing negative energy. She reached out to me, and we would talk on the phone until I realized that her conversations were demeaning. Her spirit was hateful, so I discontinued my association with her.

Oftentimes I would get into a sad mood because I had no social life or even a friend that was in my corner. Occasionally on the weekends, Saul and I would go to Waukegan to visit some of Saul's cousins. As time went on, I could see that his behavior was changing from better to worse. Saul's relatives weren't genuinely friendly towards me, and I felt disconnected from people. I didn't want to be alone, but it seemed to be the best thing. My mother wasn't especially fond of me being with her people. I believed that it was a little jealousy on her part and because she didn't know them, either. But still, she wanted somebody to look out for me. She commended me for being a clean and decent woman. She had never believed in women being friends because you had to deal with the backstabbing, fighting, jealousy, and deceitfulness. She herself was mean and ruthless if you ticked her off. But I treated all people with kindness. I was relieved that her visit was over before she could start drinking and picking fights.

Shortly after Thanksgiving I had a baby boy. The moment that I saw him, our eyes locked and joy filled my soul. He was handsome and shaped like a football star. When the doctor showed him to me, I couldn't believe that he was mine. We named him after Saul, but for short we called him J.R. I was nervous about being a mother because I didn't know what to do or how to love my baby after the past abuse I had endured. I didn't know where to start, but God showed me through grace. And then it became natural. My mother encouraged me to understand that the baby and I were growing up together. I had no other real way of looking at the matter, so I allowed my baby to grow and be free. I wanted him to grow into the person he was predestined to become. Most importantly, I didn't want to repeat that cycle of abuse.

My whole life changed from that point on. For the first time, I realized the implications of being a teen mother, but I wanted to work to support my family. I didn't have any skills, and times were up and down for us financially. Saul was laid off just about every four months like clockwork. This placed more pressure on our relationship. He would start smoking and drinking again to cope with how his life was being affected. Then he would start running the streets and hanging out. When I was alone at night, I was scared and paranoid if I heard any noises. We lived in a basement apartment, and people were always walking past our windows. Sometimes the neighborhood kids would play in the bushes and try to peep through. One time when I was lying in bed, I heard some noises coming from the bushes outside my bedroom window. There were two teenage girls watching the baby and me. Although these girls lived across the street, I felt very uncomfortable because they were always flirting with Saul.

Saul and I started having more problems because he wasn't spending enough time with me. I begin to feel very isolated, even from him. The more I complained, the more he would go and stay away at his brother's house. They would get together to drink, gamble, and talk for hours. He had grown up being very close to his siblings, but over time I began to believe that he used this as his alibi to get out the house to do other things. I never wanted to be a burden to him, so I would pray and occupy myself with the baby. But I felt like Saul was punishing me for having the baby. He wasn't ready to be a father, and an abortion would have been his excuse to get off scot-free. I had refused to do that because I had been raised to accept the consequences of my actions.

I remembered the times I would sit back and think about the three words he had said to me: "I love you." Somehow all that had changed after he'd moved to Chicago. He had made so many promises to me, going on and on about what he would do and how much in love he was with me before the baby. Now he wanted us to separate because having a family was hard on him financially. I was devastated, and I felt like he was breaking up with me because I didn't have anything to offer. I called his mother crying. She explained how he had always expressed that he loved me and dreamed of us being married one day. His problem was that he didn't want to grow up to accept his new responsibilities.

We agreed to send the baby to Saul's parents down South for the summer, but during that time I couldn't find work. Once I bought a newspaper, I realized that I didn't have any of the skills required to apply for anything that interested me. But the ones I did find interesting, I called. I ended up with a number that led me to the mayor's office of employment and training where I received a referral to learn a trade, so that I could gain some current and marketable skills.

I enrolled into a secretarial training school fall of 1986. The schooling was funded through the mayor's office, and the program paid for my lunch and bus fare to school. I chose to become a clerk typist, but I had no idea about how to type. The prerequisite to be accepted into the class was to be able to type twenty-five word-per-minute. With no other options, I prayed to the Lord to teach me how to type over the weekend.

When the coordinator, Pam, asked me to take the typing test, I told her the truth. I didn't know how to type. She sighed for a second, and then she waived the typing part of the test. She then gave me the written test only. I was admitted into the program by the grace of God; He had heard my prayer and given me favor. I started school anxiously because the next issue was getting there every day, and we only had one car. Saul would drop me off and pick me up, but that interfered when he had to look for work and take care of business.

While in the program, I met Krista, one of the other students. She taught me how to catch CTA. I used to be terrified about riding the buses; it looked so confusing and scary. I believe a lot of my fears were because I was kept locked down. And when the time came for me to grow up, it was hard. Some things came easy, but a majority of the changes in Chicago were hard. I also met Shelly and Vivian from my class. They were two wild girls. We went out for lunch one day to get something to eat, and they started smoking marijuana and drinking forties. They tried to get me to join in, but I told them I didn't drink or do drugs. They laughed, and Shelly pulled out some pictures of her boyfriend naked with a hard-on. I knew that these girls were not the type of people I needed to be getting involved with, so I slowly weaned myself away from them.

Once I finished school in the spring of 1987, I immediately started searching for a job. I was hired for the summer working in a call center at a marketing company on the North Side. I was out and about taking the buses and trains by then like a pro. I also wanted to get better at typing, so I bought an old typewriter and practiced until I got better.

When the summer ended, I applied for another job at the I.T.F.C. (In Training for Christ). I went on the interview wearing some fishnet pantyhose and a yellow and black sweater dress. My shoes were low heel. I didn't have the slightest idea of how to dress. I got pulled to the side by the Human Resource recruiter, who gave me some valuable advice. Donna candidly said that I should never wear that kind of outfit on an interview. Instead, she advised, I should wear a business outfit, preferably a suit. If I couldn't afford to buy a suit, I could find a nice one at the thrift store and take it to the cleaners. I accepted her advice, which I believed was a sign.

I prayed before taking the typing test, and I passed it. The job was contractual for only six months, but I didn't care as long as I was earning an income to support my family. During the following week I received a phone call from I.T.F.C.; they were offering me the position! I praised God for answering my prayers.

Starting a new job assured me that things were going to get better in terms of finances. Then Saul received the news that his layoff status was indefinite. Whenever this happened he would again start drinking, smoking marijuana, and running the streets. While I worked he watched J.R. because we couldn't afford to send him to daycare. I knew that he didn't want to, but money was tight. Eventually, however, I had to find someone to watch the baby while Saul searched for work.

As time progressed, I was adjusting well on my new job. And the work environment was nice. I prayed to God to help me learn my job so that it could turn into a permanent opportunity. My supervisor was quite humorous at times, and she talked a lot of mess. Rumor was that she had a drinking problem. She was tough on the staff that worked for her, but we respected her because everybody in that department wanted to become permanent. As time went on, I begin to look at the job postings on the board. I wasn't eligible until I made my six months, but during the wait I kept the faith.

One of my co-workers was from Kentucky; she and I shared stories about our Southern life. After telling her about my roots, she was amazed about all that I had been through and suggested that I write a book. I went back to my desk and images of my past flashed before me: the bullets, the long hot sunny days in the fields, riding to town on the back of my granddaddy's old Chevy truck, and watching in amazement at how my grandmother would wring the necks of the chickens we anticipated to eat for dinner. It was the freshest chicken and dumpling that I had ever tasted. I had a strange feeling that maybe I could write something that could impact someone's life in a positive way.

Saul was still having a hard time finding a full-time job. We thought that maybe the best thing to do was relocate to Birmingham, which seemed our only option if he or I didn't get a permanent job. Finally I saw a position that interested me, and I applied for it. This opportunity turned things around for us. I became a permanent employee with medical benefits to cover my family. My new boss was strict, and she managed her staff like a drill sergeant. But I realized that in this new corporate world of politics, I had to crawl before I could walk; and I hung in there as I "learned the ropes." My new position wasn't very challenging, but I was thankful to have stability in my life.

Working for I.T.F.C. prepared me for life in the corporate world. There I met Debbie. She was very polished and professional with her game, We became acquainted when I would run into her at the elevator or walk past her desk. During that time in my life I wasn't going to church or connected to any spiritual people. Debbie asked if she could talk to me about Jehovah, and I agreed. It was an awakening for me to get back involved with God. I also felt that this was an open door to meeting new people. I enjoyed talking to Debbie about God because she was very knowledgeable and patient with me. She gave me copies of *The Watchtower* and other literature. I actually learned what *Armageddon* meant. I was open to hearing about how to be a better person and learning what to do and not to do to please Jehovah. In my mind it was the knowledge to help keep me grounded.

Debbie and I started riding the train home together after work. She wanted me to give her a commitment to start studying *The Watchtower* magazine, a Jehovah's Witness preparation process to train you before your conversion to the faith. When people saw us together, they assumed that she was trying to convert me. I never minded being around her, but I wasn't sure about what kind of commitment this studying meant.

As I started to wonder about my beliefs, I began avoiding her. I started feeling pressured or coerced when we were together to hear about only Jehovah. I wanted Debbie's friendship, but I wasn't ready to commit to being a Jehovah's Witness. There was a lot to consider if I was going to do that. The things I had been taught were starting to convict me. My upbringing in the Lord and in church was quite different from the things I was hearing now about witnessing. I knew about Jesus, and I would never forget Him or stop calling on His name for all things. This witnessing just didn't rest with my soul. I knew Jesus had died on that cross for all my sins so that I could be forgiven. This stirred up feelings inside my soul about my faith. I was familiar with seeing the name *Jehovah* in the Bible, but how I had been raised to worship God was somehow going to be changed if I departed from the Holy Bible's teaching and followed this new faith. It was ingrained in my spirit to worship Jesus the Son of God. I disagreed with how Jehovah's Witnesses took matters into their own hands. If I committed a sin that was against the doctrine, I could get disfellowshipped by the elders. As a Christian, however, if I sinned or fell short, I could be forgiven without being judged by man or cast out of a faith. That was when I accepted that Jesus dying meant that I could be forgiven by His blood that was shed.

As I was leaving work one day to catch my bus, as I crossed the street on State Street and Grand Avenue, I began to envision an example Jesus gave me that brought me back to Him. The analogy was this: as I cross the street, a car comes recklessly down the street. I am not paying attention, and I can't see the danger coming my way. A man jumps in front of me to prevent the car from killing me, and he dies in the process. He made a choice to give up his life so that mine can be saved. This man has a father, who loves him deeply and unconditionally, but because of this man's loyal act of faith, I live. I am grateful to the son because of what he did. He didn't have to do it, but he cared enough for me to do it. And while I have the utmost respect towards his father, with all due respect, my praise and thanks are for the son first.

This analogy, put into my spirit by the Lord, became my reality check for coming back to Jesus. I came into an understanding of the Holy Trinity. God the Father, Jesus the Son, and the Holy Spirit are all one yoke! Every part of this trinity works together for the Glory of God. After Jesus ascended into heaven, God promised to send His Holy Spirit to be our helper leading us into all truth. If we accept Jesus into our lives, we have the spirit of truth living inside us (John 14:16-18). Then and now, I give Jesus the glory and praise because He has done great things for me when I look back over my life. I believe that the Father and the Son are real. I cannot please God if I don't acknowledge His Son Jesus. I believe and stand firm knowing without a doubt that He has done too many great things in my life to not acknowledge Him.

After my return to Christ, I realized that I was living unequally yoked in a marriage to a non-Christian. My life went down another road that became cloudy. I had chosen to marry a man that I loved, but faith was the road that I now had to journey down to find God. I had always wanted to learn how to live positively in hopes of finding a way of enriching myself. The changes that had taken place in my finding a permanent job and the career path I had chosen indicated that Jesus would always be with me even when I doubted, forgot, or made mistakes. When I evaluated my life, the things I had been taught confirmed my faith and made things clearer.

During orientation at my new job, I had also met a young lady name Paige. On my lunch hour one day we met again outside the building. She was waiting for the bus. I politely introduced myself again, and we became acquainted. We started communicating and having lunch together. We didn't talk much about the Lord in our friendship, but she was a believer, too. She was pursuing the casting business, and she shared some of her experiences about being an extra in certain movies. I was intrigued, and I asked to hear more. We talked about all types of things to do while living in Chicago, and my going to work became a lot more exciting because I had finally met someone cool and into doing fun stuff.

Paige and I planned on our lunch hour to sign up with a casting agency. I told my godsister Amaris about it, and she came along, too. She was a good friend I had met through Saul's relatives, and she had felt sorry for me when she first met me because she knew that his relatives weren't fond of me. She confided that they had told her that I was ugly and some other mean and hateful things. But she said that after meeting me, she couldn't believe my spirit and heart. We hit it off. She was fond of J.R., and she offered to babysit sometimes. I introduced her to Paige, and we all registered with the agency.

This brought me back to my fantasies of being an actress one day, which my father had shattered. Paige and I talked more and more about the business as I became more interested. She coached me on how the agency worked, which was similar to how a temporary agency worked. If they called you, and you worked on the assignment; you would get a paycheck. If you were talented or lucky, you could land a speaking part, be a stand-in, or be a principle. Also the part could bring steady work and gain you exposure. Sometimes there was food provided on the assignment, along with a chance to see the stars and maybe meet them.

Right after registering with the casting agency we were cast into a big movie, *The Velvet Box*, as extras. Then I received the phone call at work, a man asked if I could audition for a part in a movie with Greg Dakota and Frisco Lowe. I didn't know who Greg Dakota was, but I was excited about the phone call. I started asking more questions, thinking this could be my big break. But even though he called a lot, he never answered all my questions. He would only say, "I'll call you back on such-and-such a date with more details."

With all the excitement going on inside my mind, I couldn't wait to go home to tell Saul, Amaris, and my mother about the phone call. My mother was excited only because I was, but then she immediately said that it could be a hoax. Once she said that I cooled down. She was never going to be happy for me. She was very hard to convince about anything. But then she expressed that she was proud of me for trying to better myself and for raising my son.

The anonymous phone calls persisted from this man, who would never give me all the details. What I learned from each phone call I related to Paige. She advised that I get an agent. The phone calls went on for about two weeks, and I became perplexed about what was truly going on. I had no way of checking him out or tracing the phone calls because he wouldn't leave a phone number. He claimed that he was going back on his end to get more information. I started inquiring about who Greg Dakota was, and I found out that he was an Olympic swimmer.

Then my mother started asking questions about Paige. She really didn't believe that this was legit. Amaris agreed with my mother and advised me to play it out to the end. During the last conversation I remember having with this man, he insisted that I catch a plane out to Los Angeles right away. He gave some faulty information on where I should meet near the Hollywood studios, and that was how the phone calls ended. I was salty because reality had started to settle in about everything. I summed things up in my mind that this was a dirty trick. Amaris and my mother accused Paige because of her involvement in the casting business, so I confronted her and asked her if she had anything to do with the alleged caller. She denied it and asked how I could accuse her of such a thing. I told her that she knew the business, and that her best friends were the only two people capable of doing such a thing. Based on my response, she knew that I was very angry.

Amaris felt that I was really going out on a limb to continue my friendship with Paige. She and another acquaintance made mean remarks about Paige's appearance, and they assumed that she was untrustworthy because of her unattractiveness. I dismissed their comments because I knew that they didn't like her to begin with. However, I was naïve. And what I've come to know with hindsight is that people can be envious and jealous, and you will never know it. I gave it some time to blow over and continued my friendship with Paige. As time went on, we got past this; but things were shaky.

One afternoon I was in the cafeteria at work finishing my lunch when I saw a woman staring at me. I had seen her in passing out of the corner of my eye on another occasion, but I hadn't paid it any mind until she stopped me that afternoon to ask if I was her cousin. I instantly recognized her by her smile and teeth. This was the cousin my mother had introduced me to that was very negative. Her facial expression told me that she couldn't believe her eyes. Two years had passed by, and I was working and doing something positive besides being a young housewife. I didn't want to become entangled all over again with her, so I kept my answers very limited. In life there are some people whose spirits you can quickly read. Looking back over the years, I can see that God has a way of allowing people to cross my path that I felt opposition from. But of course, He always revealed the "why" of it to me at some point.

This cousin was a temporary employee, and I never saw her after our conversation that day in the cafeteria. I know that our meeting revealed that if, *God be for you then who can be against you?* With faith and perseverance you can achieve a positive change.

Paige and I started getting involved in fashion and hairstyles. On our lunch hour we would hit the stores to shop and eat. We enjoyed the walking and talking while we explored several eateries in downtown Chicago. I was working downtown around the high-rise buildings, and people were into their fashion. You could expect a new trend every season. It was the boost to get into the corporate mix of who was wearing what.

I introduced Paige to hair weave, which changed her whole look, along with other beauty tips. Paige's mother asked if I would show her how to sew the weave into Paige's hair, but there was a motive behind it. She didn't want Paige to depend on me. Amaris was angry about my willingness to share my beauty ideas. She felt that Paige and her mother only wanted to use me.

My marriage was still shaky, and there was always something going on secretly with Saul. I could never completely trust him. He seemed happy when I was off doing my own thing because it gave him more freedom to do what he wanted. He had too much free time on his hands. Eventually he found an opportunity to paint for a pastor who owned some apartment buildings around the Stony area. He paid Saul a nice weekly salary, but the only issue was that Saul had to hunt the man down for his paycheck. It's a crying shame when you're working for your people, and they get funky and string you along. This job still gave Saul too much freedom to come and go as he pleased. He had big dreams about going into business, but very little action. His plans were to start getting people under contract to ensure his income.

When I took trips out of town to visit my family, after I returned home, I would get hang-up phone calls. I always suspected that something was going on with Saul. I thought sometimes it was Saul's relatives playing tricks, disguising their voices as another woman. I knew how they felt about me; they had never given me a fair chance. Whenever I was around Saul's family, I knew that I was an outcast. But I put up with it.

I had, however, always enjoyed talking to one particular cousin. She had shown an interest in having a friendship the first time I met her. She had another sister that admired me, too. Every time I saw these girls, they would give me a hug and kiss. The age difference between us was about seven years. They admired the way that I dressed and how I wore my hair, and they were eager to babysit.

Some folks didn't like that I was getting that kind of attention. I remember one particular time I received a call from a woman who started yelling over the phone. She said to tell Saul to come get his baby, and she immediately hung up. I got angry because I didn't know what to do. I couldn't return the call and accuse anybody without knowing who it was that called. Back in those days the phone company didn't have caller ID or *69. I tried to resolve it in my mind before I asked Saul about it. I left it alone for a while, but my emotions were saying something different. I had thought that we were growing closer as a family because our finances were getting better. I started learning how to navigate my way into the corporate world. Something inside again urged me to strive for something more challenging, and I soon became unhappy with my job. I had a craving inside that pushed me to advance myself. But I knew that I had to stay in the position until things got better. So I learned how to dress better, and I sat back to watch how dirty corporate politics could get. That became my focus.



Sometimes out of the blue I felt paranoia while sitting at home waiting on Saul to return. But I suppressed my emotions by learning how to get from A to Z without being dependent on him—or anybody, for that matter, except God. I started to feel what Saul felt as a working citizen. My self-esteem grew, and I met different people on my job and in my travels. Whatever insecurity I felt with Saul, I knew that he wasn't going to leave me. I felt that our love was deep because of our history. I had his son, and we had married to secure our relationship. I vowed that I was in this for the long haul, for richer or poorer, in sickness and in health, because I loved him. These were my feelings that I based my love upon. I didn't see the truth about him because he was sneaky. He was a professional manipulator and liar.

Again there it was. Something was urging and pushing me to seek a better position within my company. I didn't possess enough skills to compete as office automation was changing. I would often hear that I needed to possess on-the-job skills such as using a fax machine, word processor, and multi-tasking. Still, I kept applying for different positions posted on the board. I had faith. I would get the interviews, but I did not get the offer. I remember getting my hopes up, and then I was disappointed every time. But again, I kept the faith and believed that something would happen for me. I read the *Daily Word* to keep me inspired.

Around late fall of 1989, my father, Jonathan, made a short visit to Chicago to move some furniture for our cousin, Faye Lynn, who had relocated there. I called her, and she put Jonathan on the phone. He spoke kindly, and then he started stuttering as he expressed that he was sorry for hurting me. He brought up excuses as to why he'd acted the way he had. This was unexpected; I had no idea that I would live to hear his confession after leaving home five years ago. I immediately told him he was forgiven.

My family and I went to visit Jonathan while he was in town. It felt awkward seeing him "around these parts." I pondered his words, but I didn't think much about him after that. I had suppressed the pain and moved on, but I knew still that I hadn't healed from the hurt. But I was able to show him love in spite of the past. I really couldn't express how I was feeling, to be honest, because my mind fell into silent shock.

After interviewing for nearly two years, I got a promotion. I started working for a "sister." I believed that I was favored because I reminded her of her daughter in some special way. In my heart I felt grateful for my new opportunity. It was more proof that God does answer prayer, over and over again. I thought this change was all I needed to get my feet on solid ground, and I was optimistic about everything. I got what I wanted in terms of more pay, flexibility, minimum supervision, and even some perks. But as I started working in the position, I realized that it wasn't a career path to open the door for greater opportunities. Still, that never discouraged me from accepting the job because I knew it was a blessing. I wanted to grow and become marketable. I had an eager attitude towards learning and being a team player.

My cousin Paris relocated from California to Chi-Town during the summer of 1990. I was excited when she came out to live here in Chicago. We had always been close from the time we were little girls, and we had stayed in touch no matter what happened in our lives. She was going through something in her life that I didn't know about, and she told me that she needed a relocation. She asked if she could come and stay with me till she got on her feet. I was all for it because we had such respect for each other, and I never felt insecure about her being around Saul. I also hoped she would occupy some of my lonely time and be good company.

My plans were to help her get a position working where I did, or assist her in seeking employment at the Federal Reserve Bank. She had strong banking skills in her work background, and I really admired her because she was ambitious, attractive, outgoing, hardworking, and had some college behind her. She drove a Mercedes, and she seemed to have her life together from the times we talked over the phone. She would send pictures to show how well she was doing. I had confidence that in no time she would be on her feet and doing her own thing.

I'll never forget the day that Saul and I went to pick her up from O'Hare airport. As soon as we all got back home, I thought that she and I were going to unwind and talk. She asked if she could go get some Baskin Robbins ice cream. I remembered that we had passed by it on the way home, so I kindly gave her my car keys. Hours went by, and after it got dark, I started to worry about her. I asked Saul to go look for her. After a day had gone by, and she was still missing in action; I was worried to death. I fell into a sleeping depression. I would come home and get straight in bed. I needed my car to get to the L station, and my cousin was still missing.

Saul and I decided that if we didn't hear back from her by the next day, we would call the police. That's exactly what we did, and they came out to the house due to the fact that my car was missing, too. They said that since Paris was twenty-one years old, the law could not do anything about her being away from home. I called her mother in California to explain and to ask if she knew anyone in Chicago besides me. Her mother said that Paris was not herself, that something was wrong with her. She confessed that Paris was using drugs. She feared that my cousin was tied up in a body bag, cut into pieces, or dead somewhere on the streets.

All of this was new to me. I had never dealt with a person on drugs with this type of behavior. I had heard that when the urge came, it was pretty intense. And that after the first hit, the cravings were twice as strong. The drug spirit ruled you and removed your old mind to replace it with a different one.

I kept praying and worrying until she showed up. She looked horrible and had lost a lot of weight. Her story was that these four guys had jumped her and taken my car. I believed her because I was concerned about her being alive at this point. She confessed that she had a disease she would be battling for the rest of her life. It was the type of disease you had to take one day at a time. She tried to be honest in expressing that once she started, she couldn't just quit. I trembled while the tears rolled down my face. I felt that our friendship had been destroyed, and the close connection we had would never be the same. She tried to convince me that she was going to get it together. We hugged each other though I was afraid to touch her, imagining how frail her bones were.

She had met a many strangers that lived nearby and in other neighborhoods, so I gave her an ultimatum: *go back to California or move out*. I knew at this point I couldn't trust her in my house. I told her that she needed to get herself together, and I couldn't help her if she was going to bring danger to my family. I was trying to get her back on the bus, but that was not negotiable. She made arrangements, and she moved out immediately. We mutually agreed that there were no hard feelings.

Paris started living with a couple around the corner. I attempted to help her get a job; somehow I felt responsible for getting her back home. She came to my job dressed up and bubbly. I notice that she was wearing a crystal charm necklace. By the way she was playing with it while she was talking; I wondered if there was any cocaine or crack inside it. She talked about the necklace giving her spiritual power and strength to find her self. I looked at her and proceeded to give her the application, but she wanted me to fill it out. She suddenly seemed exhausted and uninterested, so I suggested we take a walk over to a nearby pizzeria. While we were sitting down talking, she fell asleep. At that moment all I could remember seeing was a beautiful, intelligent, caramel-skinned woman trapped inside another world. I loved my cousin, and I had no idea what she was running from or what on earth this was all about.

At that point I ceased in assisting her with a job. She was apparently unable to get it together. I left her at the restaurant and went back to work. Later that evening Saul and I received a phone call from a man who said that he had my car. Saul asked him how he had gotten it. The man said a girl with braids had given him the car in exchange for some drugs. He was anxious to give us back the car, fearing that it had been reported stolen to the police. He ended the conversation telling us we could find the car at the L station on Ninety-Fifth Street parked inside a gas station.

Thoughts were racing through my mind; I was wondering if some of the strange man's boys would jump us or start shooting. We didn't know what the devil was going on, or what else Paris had done. I knew that I had opened a door to another set of problems and issues that I had never bargained for. I was frantic and paranoid about the whole ordeal, but Saul didn't pay it any mind.

I vaguely remembered hearing bits and pieces of a rumor in the family that Paris had gotten into some wild partying and smoking drugs. I never knew that she was attracting trouble and bringing this type of drama home. Apparently, she was "wheeling and dealing," as they call it in the streets. I couldn't focus on the things that I needed to anymore because of this negativity in my life. Paris ended up being involved with some people whom she had no business being with. She got dropped off by different cab drivers at my house. I warned her to have them drop her off at least a few blocks away because I didn't know these people with whom she was associating.

One evening I received a phone call from her calling from a pay phone. She had been abducted by a man. He took the phone from her and said he was "Scatman." I was terrified at the tone in his voice. Then he started yelling at Paris and saying he was trying to find out who I was to her. He obviously didn't believe anything she had told him. I begged him to not harm her. He said, "I'm trying to find out what her problem is." I convinced him to put her back on the phone; then I told her to pray and run!

When Paris showed up again, she told me the whole story. This man had basically kidnapped her while she was out of her mind on dope, holding her hostage. He told her that she was his now. His plans were to put her out on the streets to prostitute. He locked her up in his apartment; she couldn't get out because there were bars on the doors and windows.

While they were out catching buses one day to go buy some winter coats, they ran into his old man, who asked his son what he was doing with that pretty girl. The son was afraid of his old man. He started stuttering when he replied, but his father knew he was hiding something. He saw the fear in Paris's eyes, and he yelled at Scatman to let her go. Paris' spirit rejoiced to the Lord for hearing her cry. She started walking as quickly as she could, and as she got out of their sight, she took off running for her life and found her way back to my house.

She asked if she could wash up and spend the night. The next morning when I woke for work I told her that she needed to get her things together to leave. She had no place to go but back out on the streets. Eventually I would hear from her as she would call from different strangers' houses. I had often hear yelling and banging in the background, which caused me to cringe at the sounds of rage and danger. Paris was crying and pleading for the strength to get out of each situation. I felt afraid for her life to the point that my entire day would be messed up from worrying about her. My nerves were no good.



Saul and I ended up putting Paris on the Greyhound the next time she came to visit. We gave her no choice of coming back over if she didn't get on that bus. Things had gotten too rough and out of control. I stayed in touch with her after she made it back to California safely. She had become involved with a man who supported her, and he provided a safe place for her to stay during the times she had nowhere to go. He seemed to be very interested in her in spite of her addiction.

Meanwhile, I was trying to pick up the pieces to put my life back on track. One day after picking up my son from daycare, I was driving down 103rd Street when I heard some guys yelling. When I looked around, they pointed and screamed, "Get her!" I pressed down on the accelerator. There were four men running behind my car. I felt an eerie feeling that this was somehow associated with Paris. I panicked, unable to believe that this was happening. I was afraid for my life, trying to figure out what Paris must have done to tick these guys off. Only God knew the truth, but I believed these were the same guys Paris had hooked up with the first evening on her way to Baskin Robbins.

When they saw my car, they recognized it. Paris and I had our hair alike that summer, and people often assumed that we were sisters. I started praying.

Saul and I thought that the dust had settled after a few months. Little did we know that my car would be vandalized while parked on the street near the bus stop. Our apartment was also broken into, and we were robbed. On the day of the break-in, I had known that something was going to happen. As I was on my way out the door, I felt that someone was watching me. I had bought a London Fog coat from Marshal Field's, and I listened to my intuition that day and wore my coat to work. I thanked God that I obeyed because I would have said "bye-bye" to my nice coat.

Since our home had been vandalized, I wanted to move. But we couldn't get out of the lease. We had seven more months of living in fear of these attacks. It is true that for every action, there is a reaction. And in that situation, there was a negative reaction. I had been warned to be careful about the kind of people that I meet. This was unnecessary stress that I put myself and my family through.

When springtime arrived, we moved out of our apartment of six years and into our sister in-law's house. She lived in a better neighborhood, and we knew that we needed a new start. We planned to live with our sister-in-law for only a few months to save up to buy a home. Saul found a better job working in the suburbs. But I felt apprehensive about moving in with her because I wasn't mentally prepared. And I had suppressed my personal issues after dealing with my recent nightmare, so things started to fall apart for me at work. I fell into the "power trip syndrome" trap with my boss. We were at odds ever since I had tried to resolve some management issues with her. Some people in power feel that you need them because they have the power. This was the game that I had to play with her. I started feeling sick about being in my position. My methods to resolve this matter were failing. Our vibes were rubbing off on each other while we worked together.



I stayed professional, and I kept matters between the two of us. But it became a long-drawn-out political game. Finally I vented to my sister-in-law about the issues I was having. I didn't know how to resolve matters, but I needed to get things out. My face broke out with bad acne, and I started drinking on my lunch hour and after work. I felt useless in my job, which caused me to have low self-esteem and lack the confidence that I needed. I made the wrong move, and this was where it got me: on the black list.

Paris suggested that I move to California and find work. I started thinking that maybe I needed to relocate. It seemed to be a way out, but I wasn't certain about doing this without allowing some time to pray and plan first. I wanted to be stable with my family and do the right thing. Day after day, my thoughts grew as I fantasized about California. My aunt Vanessa had moved out there when she got divorced. She had a job and was doing well. I tried to sort things out in my mind to find balance, but I couldn't. My work and marriage were the two major causes of an enormous amount of stress in my life. Saul and I were having frequent disagreements, and we were drifting apart. I felt that things had to change, but I didn't know how to initiate the change. I wanted to run away from all the madness.

One Friday evening after work, I called home to let Saul know that I was going to stop by TGIF with a girlfriend. He seemed fine about it, but after I got home he was waiting upstairs in our bedroom. He had a strange look on his face, and I asked him what was wrong. Then he asked me where I had been. As I got closer to smell if he had been drinking, he grabbed me, putting his hands in my face. I didn't know "what-the-devil" was going on. I begin to tell him that he knew where I had been. I had told him, but somehow he wasn't listening. He pushed me down on the bed and started throwing punches while I wrestled to escape. I ran out of the bedroom towards the stairs. When I looked back he was gaining on me, and I took a leap to the bottom. I had no idea where I was running, but I made it safely inside the guest bathroom and locked the door. Saul was pulling on the door and yelling at me to open it, but I was too scared.

I had seen my sister-in-law's shadow before I made it inside. She was sitting in the den. I heard her voice, but I didn't know what she was saying. I had no idea "what- the-devil" was happening to

Saul. I could tell that he had been drinking liquor and getting high, but I was most disturbed by his behavior because it happened out of the blue. I stayed inside the bathroom all night crying and reminiscing about the times when I had to fight my father while growing up.



I was trying to cope with my issues, but it kept me off balance. I felt I was losing the battle to do right because everything seemed to be destructive. I did stay in touch with Paris, and our conversations grew more intense about my leaving Chicago. I started preparing mentally to do it. Once things simmered down, I had a talk with Saul. I started believing that if I got him away from Chicago, somehow he would not want to get high or drink so much. Surprisingly, he went along with the whole idea of relocating to California.

Paris had become pregnant while she was in Chicago, and she brought the baby back to visit the father. Her mom and my uncle drove here too, and they came by my sister-in-law's to pick up J.R. Paris and her mother had agreed to take him and watch him in California until I got there. I believed that Paris was clean and acting responsible for once in her life since having her baby. Our frequent phone calls and living with her mom assured me that someone was there in case she were to relapse. Things were falling into place, making it possible for me to get my wheels in motion. I saw no reason to stick around to fight with my job; I felt defeated. I submitted my resignation letter, and I had my exit interview with H.R. On my last day of work, my boss and her manager walked past me without speaking a word about my resignation.

Saul agreed that I should move first to get things set up, since we would be living near my family. I got packed and updated my resume. I heard much discouraging advice about the pros and cons, but I was running for more reasons than I was disclosing. When I analyzed all my problems and fears, I thought that I would be leaving them behind with this relocation. I believed with faith that I could successfully make it with God's help. On Labor Day weekend of 1991, I flew out to California.

CALIFORNIA - 1991

# CHAPTER 6

Things started off in California as though I had taken a long vacation. Paris persuaded Aunt Ernestine to allow J.R. to stay with them temporarily. Therefore, I enrolled him in the elementary school near by. This particular school was a year round school which operates on a multi-track. J.R. was assigned to track A. He was in school for three weeks and off the next three weeks. I didn't understand the logic concerning the track, but it allowed me more time to plan the next step.

I never had an official place to live. I asked Aunt Vanessa if I could stay with her for a little while. She wasn't blunt about it, but she made the comment, "I don't know about all that." I wasn't reading into her true feelings because I remembered how close we use to be. I hadn't thought any differently of her since. As a result, I was living in between both of my aunts' residences. I think that Aunt Vanessa hadn't taken me seriously when I told her that I was going to leave Chicago.

As soon as I arrived, I searched for work with every lead I could possibly find. I sent out my resumes and enlisted with the temp agency, which started calling to offer one- or two-day assignments. However they'd call the morning of and want me to report to work that same morning. Stable and permanent work wasn't surfacing.

Aunt Vanessa thought I had my expectations set too high. She felt that I should consider changing my field of work and accept whatever job came my way, but I didn't want to change my career path. I accepted the short-term assignments because my funds were getting low. I didn't have a lot of money to start out with, but I believed that my family thought differently. I knew I could always count on Saul if I had an emergency. Additionally, I had no car, and I was depending on another cousin to transport me back and forth to my assignments, which lasted for two weeks now. Her husband wasn't having it since he was left out. He had a flirtatious spirit and an ulterior motive.

Finally, I applied for unemployment, but my case was denied because I had quit my job. However, unemployment placed a condition on my situation. I had to work part-time consistently for four weeks in order to qualify for benefits. That became unattainable based on no job openings within the area. Things started looking hopeless at that point. I was facing two dilemmas. I had no residence or car. Aunt Vanessa was keeping her cool and waiting to see what my plans were, but she started insinuating that I needed to pay some rent. She obviously didn't believe that I would have moved without having a stash of money. I wasn't used to her treating me this way because we had always been there for one another.

Aunt Vanessa enjoyed partying. She had changed a great deal after her divorce. Once she moved to California, she possessed a lustful spirit that caused her to talk loosely about sex. I didn't see that in her behavior until I spent time around her. Now it had become a part of her personality. She was candid about expressing her point of view, and she didn't want to listen to my personal concerns or needs at this point. I knew that time was winding down for me to face up to where I was going with this move. The bouncing back and forth was becoming tiresome. My focus changed in my search for work; I needed to get a car.

In between waiting for something permanent and stable to come along, I was falling into a more confused state of mind. Paris would say things to inspire me to not give up, but I was losing my faith. Her mom couldn't offer me a place to live because she was occupying a room on her in-laws' property. Their home was actually a group home for mentally ill patients. My aunt Ernestine worked there, and she had Paris, the baby, J.R., and my uncle living there.

I called Saul to explain that I needed a car and about my living situation. I expressed that things weren't looking good. He sent me money to buy a reliable beater, but I decided to wait because I was afraid of getting a lemon. Because of the way things were going, I started thinking pessimistically.

Paris got her car repaired, and we started hanging out. I met a few of her friends. I was impressed to meet some cool people who worked professional jobs and had nice cribs. But, as they say, birds of a feather flock together. Some of Paris' friends were into drinking alcohol, getting high, scheming, and cursing. We went clubbing a few times at Paradise 21, a club well known to attract celebrities. One evening while we were hanging out at the club, Jodeci performed. I remember back in the day when Paris would call to tell me stories about whom she had met and what she was doing. She sounded very excited. I wondered sometimes about how differently my life would have been if I hadn't gotten married young.

Paris was attending school part-time at the community college. When her school check arrived, she said, "Let's go to the mall." I was cool with that because I hadn't received any news regarding work. I felt like my life was going nowhere; my time wasn't being utilized correctly, and the weeks were passing by quickly. From my observation, Paris seemed to be functioning normally—at least that's what I thought.

Riding home from the mall, she made a confession that she had stolen a pair of pants. I was in shock, and I didn't know what to say because she had just gotten a nice check. She was acting as if it didn't faze her; I could actually see the excitement in her eyes. She immediately conjured up another plan to go back the next day, telling me that she wanted to steal more merchandise. I tried to discourage her from doing it, but she just asked me to keep the baby in case she got caught. I went along with it because I knew that I wasn't going to steal anything.

She shoplifted at the same store from the night before and got arrested by security. I saw my life heading for big trouble because I was hanging around a person I didn't understand and apparently didn't know. I had never had any intentions of moving to California to become a thief or get a record. I had credit cards and credit available to charge anything that I could afford within my means. I knew from my past where stealing had gotten Lionel. I often thought about his life and how different it could have been if he had listened.

Again, I attempt to explain the scenario to Saul. And I complained that things weren't working out, and that I wanted to come home. He convinced me to stay because he was coming. The weather was getting cold, and the season had changed. There were hardly any warm, sunny days like when we hung out by the pool. It was going on six weeks, and things weren't working according to my plans. Saul was giving me excuses about why I should stay because he was concerned about what his job would think if he reneged. Meanwhile I was being hammered by Aunt Vanessa for rent. She felt that I was out and about having fun with Paris, and I realized that she and Paris had become running buddies after her divorce. Let me correct that by saying, they were partners in crime. They were into some wild things that I had not even dreamed of. I eventually paid her fifty dollars to get off my back. I had my things stored at her place. But I was mindful not to eat her food, and I contributed to helping with chores, the kids, and favors when she asked. I felt pressure from her about the fact that I wasn't able to give more, even though I had paid for all of her expenses whenever she wanted to visit me in Chicago. My mother had tried to warn me about her; she felt that Aunt Vanessa was a user. Her feelings were strong about this, and it turned out she was right.

Finally I went beyond the area to search for work as well. I remembered visiting family on my mother's side in Sacramento back in 1990. They seemed happy to see me during my visit, but maybe that was because I hadn't seen them since I was a little girl. This was my mom's sister, Shelly, Shelly's daughter, and her children. I decided to give my cousin Tracey a call to ask if her offer of a temporary place to stay still stood. I was up front with her about my failure to find a job, and she welcomed me anyway to stay with her for a temporary period of time. I dragged J.R. out of school, and off we went on the Greyhound.

Immediately after we arrived at the bus terminal, I could tell that things weren't going to pan out. I wanted to go back to Chicago. In my mind I could hear Saul saying that things would be better here and to at least try it. So I went through another ordeal, which turned out to be worse. Tracey had a toddler living with her, and her one-bedroom apartment was too small to accommodate the four of us. I knew that I didn't have much time if I was going to make this work. So I started off with a serious drive to find employment. I didn't honestly know my cousin as well as I thought. Occasionally her boyfriend would stop by. I tried to give them their privacy, but I felt uncomfortable with all of the adjustments, so I tried to exhaust myself by looking for work.

Eventually I fell into the routine of tagging along with Tracey and her boyfriend. The times that I wanted to stay at home she would insist that I go. Tracey had a kind spirit, spoke properly, and carried herself professionally, but I sensed a sneaky side to her. I believed that I had worn out my welcome when we started having disagreements and arguments. I felt bad because I started feeling like I was a burden. When I first met Tracey's boyfriend, he was kind and friendly. He would make suggestions to her about doing fun things that included me. I thought he was cool. So I started having small conversations, just talking about Chicago, and being friendly, too. Whenever he'd come over, I would either go into the bedroom; or they would. When they'd come out, I would make remarks and look at them as though I knew what they were doing. Her boyfriend would either smile or say something back as a joke, but Tracey didn't like it. I didn't realize that I rubbed her the wrong way.

Aside from the fact that I was out there away from Saul, they started wondering about my situation. Tracy went to the extreme of setting me up with one of her boyfriend's friends. Her boyfriend picked us up one evening for dinner with his friend in the car. I analyzed the picture. I was quiet and mannerable because I could tell that I was being watched. I wasn't tempted to commit adultery though. I knew about the consequences. Plus, I wasn't crazy, knowing that I could be blackmailed.

We left dinner to go dancing at a nightclub. I danced with the guy, but to me that was all it was: a dance and dinner. This man started asking questions about Saul and why I had moved. Once that night came to an end, I wanted to get out of Tracey's house.

My next move was to see if I could persuade Venus, Tracey's sister, to sympathize with me. She was receptive to my conversation, and I didn't have to convince her that it was difficult living with Tracy. I asked if I could stay with her, and she kindly agreed. I knew it was my opportunity to leave Tracey's before we fell out. I stayed with Venus for approximately three weeks. She was expecting her second child, and she had a two-bedroom apartment. We got along because there weren't any men hanging around or negativity, and we were good company to each other because our spirits were compatible. Also Venus didn't drive, so she didn't get out that much.

After enrolling J.R. in kindergarten and getting him off to school, I was in pursuit of finding my way. Sometimes I would walk for miles to make it to my destination. One afternoon on my way to pick J.R. up from school, I met Savanna. We spoke in passing, and for some reason, we had a small conversation while waiting outside for the bell. Our kids were in the same classroom, and we discovered that we both were from Detroit. We hit it off very well from that point on, sharing our stories about what had brought us out to California. She said that her husband was in the military, and then we exchanged phone numbers. Savanna lived within a few blocks from Venus.

During my two weeks of living with Venus I didn't feel the pressures that I had experienced with Aunt Vanessa and Tracey. I stayed focused and determined to search every day for work. I put in job applications all over the city, and eventually I got hired at the junior college. There was one small dilemma: I couldn't start work until January fourth due to the effective date for the new budget. The wait was six weeks before I could start. I was happy about the news, but on the other hand I was still a sitting duck. I decided to be wise by not stopping there with my job search.

Tracey started calling Venus to stir up the pot, treating her mean because things were working out between us. Saul called Tracey's, not knowing that I had moved, and Tracey insinuated bad things about me to him. She came by to pick up Venus to take her grocery shopping, and I asked if I could go. After making two stops, Tracey and I got into an argument. She stopped the car and put me out. She wanted to punk me around because I wouldn't kiss her behind. I understood that I was in her car, but there was still a right and wrong way to treat somebody.

After that incident, Venus turned on me. She depended on her sister for all her outside care. And to show her loyalty, she had to be stern and shake things up. Once again my wheels were spinning in the wrong direction. I prayed and asked God to help me. I didn't want to give up at this point because I had felt that I could make it.

Tracey gave me some mail that came to her address, which turned out to be a check from I.T.F.C. I'm sure that if she had known that it was a check, I would never have gotten it. I was planning to use the money for an apartment and a car, but now I didn't know which way to go. I started venting to my mother and explaining to her about what was going on. She told me to go back home, and she started getting uptight and using profanity. I regretted asking for her advice. I pawned my jewelry to get more cash, and I prayed, knowing that more money could change my situation.

Savanna, my newest friend here in California seemed to be a kind and friendly person from my observation. She and her family invited J.R. and me out for pizza. She asked if my family would be okay if I spent time with her and her family, and I replied "yes." I thought my cousins could care less as long as I wasn't bothering them. So for Thanksgiving, J.R. and I ate dinner with Savanna's family. When we returned home to Venus' that evening, however, I discovered that all of our things were missing. Tracey was nonchalant when I asked what was going on. I pleaded and begged for answers regarding my things, but somehow I assumed that it was all a trick. Venus refused to talk, so I got furious and ran out the door searching for a policeman. I waved at a passing police car, and he stopped the vehicle to see what was wrong.

He questioned Tracey and Venus about my things and their relationship with me. Venus kept quiet while Tracey did all the talking. The officer didn't like the way Tracey was talking, so he checked her and asked for permission to walk through the apartment. But of course my things weren't there. I explained to the officer that I was from Chicago, and that I had relocated to be around my family. The police suggested that I take this matter to the small claims court if my cousins refused to return my things. I knew that could take months, and by that time my thoughts would be far away from there. So I got on the phone and asked my mother to have Aunt Shelly talk to them.

Shelly called immediately to intervene. She asked why they were being ugly. "God don't like ugly," she said. Aunt Shelly had a sweet and peaceful spirit. She spoke slow and always greeted family with a hug and kiss. Her favorite words were *sugar* or *baby, how you doing* with this big smile. But Venus and Tracey weren't hearing that mushy talk because they wanted to punish me.

The more that I became entangled in this web of deception, the more I realized that time was running out. Tracey told Aunt Shelly that she didn't like the way that I talked around her boyfriend, and that I had a smart mouth. Saul finally called to find out why they were holding my things. They told him that I had been running the streets and hanging out, but he knew that wasn't my behavior. I was so frustrated from all the mind games. I was at the mercy of Savanna's help. I stayed with her at that point because I was no longer welcome at Venus'.

The phone calls went on for a day or two before things came to an end. Tracey stated that I owed her money for rent and a phone bill. I apologized and paid my debt in full in exchange for my things. I had to learn to walk in humility and patience while I endured another nightmare from the pit. In conclusion, it was about the money. I am not a user, and if there's anything that I want, I will work or ask for it. I was mindful whenever I used any of my cousins' amenities, and I asked for their permission. I was aware of any expenses that I utilized. I was steaming with rage and anger about how I had been double-teamed. I knew that it was time to move on, and there was nothing that Saul could say to prolong my stay. I thanked God for my meeting Savanna, who had made sure that J.R. and I had a place to stay.

A few days later we got packed and I bought food for our departure. Savanna drove us to the bus station. When it came time to say good-bye, I expressed my gratitude with all my heart. Through my ordeal a bond was formed between us. Savanna is a woman that exudes beauty, wisdom and grace. I felt honored to see how she balanced her life and caring for her family. We are still friends today through this connection. God had sent her into my life to be that guardian angel until my steps became straight. I stared out the window while the bus drove off, anticipating the long journey as a time to reflect and sort things out in my mind. As I drifted far away inside, my thoughts became images that reflected the scenes of my life.

God knew that I didn't know what to expect back in Chicago because I wasn't willing to accept my failures. I had so much on my mind, bridges to cross, and some sense of direction to regain. I even wondered if I still had a marriage waiting for me in Chicago. While I was away, I had stayed in touch with Amaris, the only person with whom I could share my faults and failures. She always reminded me of the good, and she held me in high regard. We became closer friends through my troubles and struggles.

I was in search of a new life, which I believed was out there somewhere. I wanted better for myself and running away wasn't the answer. I had to consider the fact that I was a wife and mother. My poor son had been dragged across the country and had attended two different schools. We finally arrived downtown Chicago three days later during the week of Christmas.

Illinois - 1991

# CHAPTER 7

J.R. and I were looking forward to being at home. Saul and I found an apartment in the suburbs. And I was blessed with a new job, even though I took a four-dollar cut in pay because anything was better than being without an income. But we encountered a new problem: childcare. The fees were equivalent to the cost of a one-bedroom apartment. We had to figure out a plan to make this move work, so we agreed to send J.R. to live temporarily in Alabama. Paying for him to go to kindergarten a half day and then to daycare wasn't worth it.

My soul was weary, and I needed rest. I felt content to be left alone inside my own four walls of solitude. It didn't matter to me that we didn't have a phone for a while. My thoughts were serene for the first time since the last apartment. I thanked God for Amaris, who was very supportive.

At first I wasn't watching Saul's pattern or paying any attention. I started noticing that he wasn't content being at home; he was running into the city every other day and on the weekends. I had stopped caring about what he was doing because I had suppressed my true feelings about whether he was cheating on me or not. I was trying to find my independence again in the workforce. Therefore, my marriage was not my main focal point. The truth was, I wasn't emotionally ready to deal with my marriage. What could I change? I couldn't face knowing what I didn't want to hear.

I knew I was limiting myself sitting behind a switchboard, so I still struggled to gain more competitive skills for the job market. I knew I had the potential to do better than answering phones. But this kind of work always fell into my lap and kept food on my family's table. I wasn't content, so I continued to send out my resumes. I prayed and kept searching for a better job. Our finances were always in trouble if I didn't work because Saul was a bad money manager. He had a gambling addiction, and at times he'd go straight to the casino on payday before coming home. He blew his money on a lot of booze and nonsense. Saul had never quit his job while I was going through these transitions.

Finally I saw an ad in the paper for a receptionist/ secretary position at a pharmaceutical company. I felt differently about this opportunity because it offered secretarial duties along with PC training. I went into deeper prayer by fasting and preparing as I kept the faith to believe in God for the outcome.

During the interviewing process, I was informed that it would take a few weeks before they reached a decision. I was hoping for an answer sooner. In the meantime, I was still working at my current job. On one particular day I transferred a call to the wrong extension, which happened to be the owner's son. He came running over to my desk and started yelling. I immediately got angry because I felt embarrassed and stupid. It was his ignorance, not mine. I asked a co-worker to relieve me, and I went to the washroom. As soon as I entered the washroom, I burst into tears and cried out to the Lord to rescue me. At this point I made up my mind to quit, but I waited to finish the week out. I couldn't take anymore negative outbursts or comments. I felt threatened that I couldn't make a mistake without serious consequences. Working in that type of environment was unhealthy, and it could cause me to become bitter. It was only a paycheck to get me back on my feet. On my last day of work, I kept a smile on my face. And at the end of the day, I cleared my desk and never looked back.

While waiting to hear back from the pharmaceutical company, I started getting a lot of hang-up calls at home. I didn't think much about it because it was during business hours. Then I got a call one evening from a guy asking to speak to Saul. I had never heard this person's voice before, so I asked who was calling. He wouldn't tell me his name. I politely gave Saul the phone. Saul didn't want to talk in front of me. He walked around, and then he went into another room. That's when I started getting suspicious about him being secretive. I would act as though I wasn't paying any attention, asking, "Oh, who was that?" He would give me a name and change the subject or get quiet. I knew he wasn't telling the truth.

One afternoon I fell asleep, and I had a vision that I was exchanging words with the pharmaceutical company. I woke feeling tired and started thinking about the reality of my life. Suddenly the phone rang. It was the pharmaceutical company calling to offer me the position. I eagerly accepted the job, and I thanked Jesus for answering my prayer. Before I got off the phone, the recruiter mentioned that I would get another salary increase after my ninety days. That's when I really got excited.

I started working in March of 1992, and I couldn't believe that the other employees were genuinely nice, friendly, and professional. I could feel the high morale in that work atmosphere. I received compliments on how I dressed and on my professionalism, which made a big difference in my attitude when I came to work.

But my marriage was falling apart day by day. I felt this piercing on the inside that I couldn't seem to shake from my heart. After being at my job for about two weeks, I received a call at the switchboard from a woman asking to speak to me. She said she had a child by Saul, and he was afraid to tell me. She admitted that she had been calling my house and hanging up because she knew that I didn't know anything about the situation. I tried to hold my composure together, feeling heat rising like a thermometer in my face. I was speechless from being in shock, but finally I asked her how long this affair had been going on and what proof she had that Saul was the father. She said the baby had a country accent. I could tell from this reply that she was trash, and I told her that it wasn't proof.

Calls were coming through on the switchboard, and my emotions were going crazy, so I hung up on her. I immediately called home to confront Saul about the matter. I could tell that he was expecting my call because he answered the phone as though he was surprised to hear my voice. I gave him the news about my conversation with Ms. Doe. He replied with a laugh. I said some mean, nasty, and hateful things to him, and I told him that we had trouble if this was true. I realized that I was falling apart, and it was time to leave work.

As soon as I got home I demanded that Saul talk to me. He knew I was furious and that I needed to know what the hell was going on. I could tell that he had been getting high and drinking. I was extremely hurt, and here he had the audacity to get high! I demanded that he give me this woman's number and tell me that it wasn't true. He gave me her number, so I could talk to her. He wouldn't discuss the matter. When I called her, we went back and forth over the phone; and I was still only getting her version of the story. Again I felt like I was getting nowhere, so I got off the phone. It was useless; this was not my mess. But somehow I realized that it *was* mine, too. I had married him. I became full of rage; heat started circulating to the top of my head. And by this time, I couldn't talk any more. I was moving around like an uncontrollable maniac. I poured a glass of Jack Daniels straight and grabbed the Tylenol and Tetracycline bottles. Then I ran into the bedroom, threw all the pills down my throat, and washed them down with eight ounces of liquor. Saul tried to stop me, but it was too late. I slipped into a moment of insanity because I couldn't make sense of anything. My emotions and thoughts were confused. I needed to escape because I couldn't calm down. My world came crashing down instantly; it felt like explosions were going off inside my head. I couldn't be still; I had enough strength to kill someone, that's how angry I was. Trust me, I know what it feels like to be lost within that moment of insanity.

While my volcano was erupting, Saul was sitting at the dinner table acting nonchalant. He said that he couldn't run anymore from this woman. Time was running out with his lies because she had reported him to public aid. The state sent papers to his job to garnish his check for child support. I believe that was when he knew she wasn't going away. He said he'd given her money to have an abortion. It was now obvious to me that he had been dodging and running from this woman for years because I remembered the phone call from a woman demanding that he come get a baby. I didn't completely believe that this woman had been behind every single hang-up call, but it certainly revealed that she had her motive. Saul confessed that he was giving her money for this child. I found out that he had given her my baby's red hotshot car, a sentimental gift from my mother. I had realized it was missing after we moved. When I had asked him about the car, he'd said that he'd given it away to a cousin when I moved to California. Saul was a master at lying, and of course I loved him. I couldn't see through his lying spirit—or maybe I truly didn't want to.



This woman who alleged that he was her baby's father said that she had tried on several occasions to convince him to tell me about the affair because she knew it was driving him crazy. He was afraid I might leave him, and he didn't love her. So he basically was caught. I was exhausted at this point, and I decided to stop talking. I couldn't handle any more news in one day. Saul suggested that we lie down and take a nap. I tried to fall asleep, but my mind was too confused. I had never felt so much anger at one time in my entire life. I couldn't calm down, even though liquor usually makes me sleepy. I remember getting up to read one of my *Daily Word* books to find some comfort of hope. Inside I found an 800 number for prayer twenty-four hours a day. I decided to call the number since the call was free. I talked to a live person, a mild-mannered woman who sounded like she was reading from a script because her demeanor was too pleasant and her voice was soft spoken. My thoughts were too scattered to hold a conversation, and my mind fell into this dark place of despair. I told her that I was full of anger and asked her to help me.

After she prayed for me, I hung up the phone and called Amaris.

Amaris knew immediately that I was hiding something. My voice was slow, and my speech was slurring. She started to fish for answers, and I told her that I had taken some pills. She screamed and told me to put Saul on the phone. I woke him up and gave him the phone. After talking to her, he immediately took me to the twenty-four-hour emergency center. I had my stomach pumped, and I was taken to the hospital in the ambulance. I stayed in intensive care for a day. I wasn't afraid of what I had done; I wanted to die. My heart was heavy like a ton of bricks had fallen on me. All I could think about was the betrayal, and the embarrassment I had to face. I felt horrible and trapped inside.

Saul called my job to report my absence and tell them I was in the hospital. The job asked if they could send flowers, but he said "no" because he was too embarrassed that they might find out why I was there. One of our cousins-in-law called to speak to me. And when Saul informed her that I was in the hospital, she came to visit me. She sensed that something was wrong from the last time we spoke. I felt ashamed and embarrassed. I didn't want anybody to see me in that situation or state of mind, with tubes stuck down my nose and throat. Saul could have spared me the embarrassment, but he didn't. This cousin wanted to know what had happened, but I wouldn't disclose the truth to her. I wasn't ready to accept the truth at that time, and I didn't want her spreading rumors in case it turned out to be untrue about Saul's child. I had enough stuff to deal with during this tumultuous time.

The doctor informed me that if I hadn't made it to the hospital by the time I did, I would have died within another hour due to liver failure. I had to attend a group to discuss my hurt. I spoke with a psychiatrist about why I had attempted suicide, explaining that I was afraid of facing my fears, and I didn't think I could freely live my life without feeling ashamed and humiliated. He recommended that I go to college to attain some type of degree that would make me eligible for a profession.

On my way home from the hospital I felt disconnected from the world. This experience of being locked up physically against my own will caused me to think differently in terms of being out-of-touch with reality. The outside world seemed foreign for a minute, I believe, because my spirit was grieved. The flowers that my job had sent to my home were beautiful, but I couldn't appreciate them because I had no joy inside. I wore a mask back to work. It felt like a piece of my soul was missing; I was empty.

Saul and I had begun to discuss his affair and his alleged child. I was very sensitive about the subject, but I had to face it in order to know the truth. The truth can reveal things that can either hurt you or release you, and I wanted my soul to be set free of this agony. Baby Doe's mother continued to call to complain about the child needing this and that; she expected Saul to buy whatever she needed. She started throwing her weight around because she felt that there were no more secrets now. And she wanted to punish him for having to raise the child alone. That's why she had pushed the issue to have him served with court papers. Once the state got involved, Saul was subpoenaed to establish paternity. He ignored the court, but I told him that he had better deal with the issue. I told him that if it was his child, I was leaving, because this was mentally and emotionally tearing me apart.

Saul was served with another set of court papers to respond to the allegations, or else he would be automatically determined as the father. Finally he stepped up to the plate to comply. I thought the matter was going to be resolved right away, but that wasn't the case. Ms. Doe was hoping that Saul and the baby would bond by building a relationship, so she offered him visitation. I told him that before he started doing anything like that he'd better be certain that this was his child. He expressed that he had some doubt about being the father. He added that the day he'd driven to her place to give her the abortion money, she had gotten into another man's car. Then they pulled off, laughing, and obviously she hadn't gotten the abortion.

My thoughts about the matter were that she believed he had something to offer her besides child support. Or maybe she wanted to trap him in case she could get something later. I had my phone number changed, and I told him to deal with the court. I didn't have the strength to make any decisions about whether I should stay or leave. I had recently gone through so much that by this time. I was fragile.

As time went on, I tried to resume my life. But my trust in my husband was shattered. I fell into a mild depression for a few months, and I cried every day when I came home from work. I would go into my bedroom and feel sorry for myself because the pain was piercing. I saw gray clouds for days because I couldn't appreciate the sun.

Eventually the tears stopped falling. I started walking with my head up as I trained myself to stop loving Saul. I was able to stop the flow of loving him deeply. I stayed because I didn't believe that I could make it on my own. Our relationship went in a different direction. We started having family dinners and throwing parties. I got involved in smoking pot and drinking my share of liquor, too. I went along with this lifestyle because I had no more dreams and hopes about anything.

From my early years growing up with my parents, I saw what liquor and drugs did to their lives. I didn't want to end up like that, looking bad and physically worn out. This was the boundary I placed within my mind. We enjoyed our fun within our social circle. We would get high, eat, and drink together, but when the party was over the misery was still there. I decided to start exercising after being insulted by a neighbor who thought that I was pregnant with twins. The alcohol had started putting the weight on me, so I knew I had better get a grip on things. I had an unforgettable experience one day while smoking marijuana. I started choking on my smoke, and my heart started racing. I couldn't catch my breath. Then I called on the name of Jesus, and eventually my lungs got clear. I calmed down, and my mind fell into a trance. After I came to, I decided to stop smoking. I didn't want to die like that and meet God in that kind of way. I needed to stop pleasing Saul. He enjoyed me getting high and being freaky with him. I complained that this behavior was putting pressure on me, and it wasn't of God. I couldn't conform any more to what Saul wanted.

J.R. was back at home with us after finishing kindergarten in Alabama. Saul's niece came to babysit for the summer while we worked. Our plan was working out with having our son home. By the time we sent his niece back to Alabama, J.R. would be ready to start first grade. Having J.R. in school all day was a huge relief financially to us.

Around this time, we went visiting over at Saul's brother's house in Altgeld Gardens. One of their neighbors came over while we were visiting. Saul grabbed her by the hand, and their eyes met. He looked at her from top to bottom. Everybody stopped talking and stared at this sudden act. I didn't say anything right away because I couldn't believe my eyes. Then I asked him what that was all about, and he told me that he was trying to hook her up with his nephew. I told him he was totally disrespecting me, and his nephew was a grown man who could find his own woman. He started talking loudly and being nasty. I told him that I was ready to go, and then I told J.R. and Saul's niece to go get in the car. Saul started driving recklessly because he was too high and drunk. We had an hour and fifteen minute drive going home. His niece started screaming for me to drive, but I wouldn't take the wheel. Then Saul pulled over off the expressway to puke. I made everyone suffer because of my anger.

After we made it home in one piece, Saul parked the car. Then I started talking about the incident, but he ignored me. I guess he didn't want our neighbors to hear me go off. Once we got inside the house, I went into the kitchen to get a long butcher knife. I started waving it at him and aimed it at his chest. He had this grin on his face like he wasn't feeling me. As I got closer his niece screamed, "Run, Saul!" He ran out the front door and down the stairs, and he stayed with the neighbors for the rest of the night.

The next day he packed his clothes, and he talked about going to go live with his brother in New Mexico. I felt miserable, but somehow I think he used the leaving tactic to reverse the psychology. We both were living dysfunctional lives. He had a sickness that I couldn't see, and I was an abused woman. Eventually I lost weight, and things were still going well at work. Then I got the news that I was pregnant. I wasn't happy about that because it got in the way of my hopes of leaving Saul. Would I ever be able to break free from this unhealthy relationship? I couldn't see how, not with two babies. I felt like a spider trapped inside a web.

It was summer of 1993 when I got a phone call that my mother was in the hospital in San Francisco. She had left Michigan to visit her sister, who lived in the Bay Area. The story that I heard was that some guys had jumped her outside the bus terminal and robbed her. She had been beaten very badly from the way the doctor described it, but the hardest part was discovering that she had a terminal illness. My heart felt heavy. Although she acted rough and tough like she could handle any situation on her own, this time I believed that she was seriously hurt. She was diagnosed with cancer, and the doctor decided to give her chemo treatments because her cancer was in its advanced stage. The final prognosis about her health was that she had only a year to live.

My family in Sacramento wanted to reach out, but I wouldn't. Instead I contacted my aunt Honey who lived in Michigan. She and my mother had fought for many years, but she ended up being the one who was there to do the administrative part of getting her flown back to Michigan. I had planned three trips to Michigan over the course of time, and I had phone conversations in between my visits with my mother. Her conversations were shorter each time because she was growing weaker. I could tell that she wasn't used to being humble, but for the first time in my life I saw it happening. It's a true statement, but not often recognized. An illness can make you humble. Her health was deteriorating day by day; she was regressing back to infancy. I felt especially bad when she lost all her hair because she was such a hair person. She cared a lot about her appearance. But after living a hard life, she was robbed of her beauty and health.

Meanwhile, I was trying to hold onto my sanity through my own hellish marriage. I had remorseful feelings about being pregnant. I did have some good days, but the majority of them were bad. Saul was putting me through all kinds of hell, staying out late and coming home at disrespectful times. He was working the evening shift and getting off at midnight, and he would tell me that he didn't see a reason to come straight home after work since I was asleep. Things were beyond resolution, so I addressed what I could and suppressed what I couldn't.

On January 23, 1994, I gave birth to our second son. I went through the postpartum blues, wondering why I couldn't have just died. I resented my baby, and I hated my marriage. But there was still something inside that gave me hope to believe that my life was going to change. I couldn't see how or when, but I had enough faith to keep praying. I tossed and turned in agony, but I found that prayer was my greatest hope. The Lord knew that I was tired of the pain.

Finally I came to realize that I loved both of my kids, and that God had given them to me for a reason. I felt overwhelmed by all these new responsibilities and dilemmas, but there was something special about Jacob. Wherever we would go, he would attract attention. He smiled all the time, and he was a happy baby. The Lord blessed him indeed with a charm that allured others. His uncle even gave him the nickname "Happy." I couldn't see why, because I was always miserable.

While my mother was dying she was desperately trying to reach out to me. She would have someone dial my number, so she could hear my voice. I felt sad because I couldn't be there in person to hold her hand. I never felt guilty about what I couldn't do because I couldn't be all things to all people. But I kept her in my prayers, and I asked God to comfort her mind with peace.

During May of 1994, I arranged a trip to visit her for Mother's Day. During the visit I talked about the Lord, and I asked her if she believed in God. She replied that she did. I asked her if she wanted to hold my baby, but she declined. I felt she didn't want to create that bond knowing she wouldn't be able to see him grow up. I do recall a special moment while sitting next to her. She leaned over and whispered into my ear. The fumes that came from her insides indicated that she didn't have much longer to live. In life some aromas are unforgettable, but this one haunted my soul. While we were bonding, Aunt Honey decided to go for a walk. But as she walked towards the door, she turned around. My mother had a disturbing look on her face that caused Honey to stay in the room to eavesdrop.

In that moment my mother couldn't muster up the wind to repeat her words. I could only hear broken whispers. She was trying to tell me her last wishes. She nodded her head to be polite. Saul couldn't handle seeing her that way, so he said that he was going to take a smoke. My mother heard the word *smoke,* and she went berserk for a cigarette. Aunt Honey told her "no." It was the last thing that she needed. But my mother started moaning while her eyes screamed for one. Her spirit became sad when we got ready to say "good-bye." She expressed her love for J.R. by whispering desperately for Aunt Honey to give him some money. Honey replied that she would give him some, but we never saw it.



A week later my cousin called to inform me that my mother had asked for me again, but I couldn't break away to fulfill her request. My cousin, at least, was there to give her some comfort. I prayed because there was nothing else that I could do. Three weeks after that I received a phone call at work from Aunt Honey. I sensed immediately that something was wrong. I could tell by the tone in her voice that it was time. I cried at that moment, informed my job of the news, and I left work. Tears were streaming down my face while I drove home.

My mother died on her sister's birthday. I carried a heavy heart around and lay awake at night just thinking. It doesn't matter how close you are to your parents; it hurts when they die. They are a part of you regardless of how good or bad they were. And when they die, a part of you dies, too. You are connected in the spirit and through your genes. I've always been told that I laugh like my mother, and that I favor her. Sometimes I can see it, and it frightens me because I never wanted to be anything like her.

We immediately planned for the funeral. I was anxiously contemplating the fact that I was going to see family I hadn't seen since I was a little girl. Aunt Honey stepped in to take care of the funeral arrangements. When I viewed my mother's body, I couldn't believe my eyes; she looked beautiful. While she was alive, she had endured a hard and violent life. As she got older, it had shown on her face. I have no pictures of my mother to remind me of her sad life because I decided to hold her last look as my best memory. Rocky was there, but Lionel was unable to attend because we couldn't afford his bail. I know that he had to feel terrible to have missed his mother's funeral, but there wasn't much we could do at that point. Lionel was my mother's heart; she had spoiled him and loved him very much. She was fighting for his freedom until the day of her tragedy. And even at that point, she was unable to give him any mental support. She would pawn her jewelry and other items to do whatever she needed in order to put money on his books. My mother's dying meant a lot to Lionel. I believed that she was the only soul in this world that truly loved him. She was his only source of hope, besides God.

My Uncle Steve commented at the repast that "...at least we don't have to worry about where Bunny's at." I knew exactly what he meant by it. I didn't take any offense. Her family couldn't do anything with her while she was growing up. She had a rebellious spirit and was very hard-headed. I only knew my mother's side of the family up to age six. We would go visiting our aunts and uncles to celebrate the holidays, and my mother would start drinking and get into a fight. I don't know if it was due to her temperament, mental illness, or the alcohol.

My mother had never wanted her side of the family to raise us. I believe that she had her reasons, and they were probably valid ones. I felt that her family was observing my behavior to see if I had her spirit. I am not perfect, that I understand. But due to God's mercy over my life I was blessed.

In conclusion they noted on her obituary that, "*Bunny was a lover of life*." Rocky behaved at the funeral. I made sure that I wasn't left alone with him because he talks a lot of foolish talk. It's only a matter of time before he starts clowning. Give him one drink, and it's on. Unfortunately he was the one who inherited both our parents' temperament and alcoholic genes.

Less than two months later I received a phone call from Rocky. He asked me to buy our mother's headstone. I could tell that he had been drinking because he wasn't listening to what I had to say. I tried to talk sensibly at first until I saw where he was coming from, so I hung up the phone. I grieved in silence as I persevered to balance my new responsibilities.

I started my exercise regimen again. I wasn't happy about my weight after the baby because I had gained seventy-five pounds. I stayed focused on managing my responsibilities and making time for my workouts in the evenings. I was well on my way to dropping the pounds. One evening I heard a knock at the door while I was working out. It was a woman that lived in my apartment complex. Her son and J.R. were playmates at school. She wanted to introduce herself to make sure that her son was welcome in my home. I stopped the video to catch my breath while I talked to her. She seemed pleasant and concerned like most parents, and I assured her that it was fine if her son came over to visit.

When I went back to work after maternity leave, the company had hired a new staff of managers. That's when things started going downhill. Management enforced a new set of rules, which affected the morale in the work environment. There were only two African American women that worked there, as well as two men. One of the women, Jasmine, shared her news about her promotion, and I was happy to hear that one of us had gotten advanced for a change. When I was on leave she brought me a print-out of all the job openings. I saw a position that I felt qualified for, and I applied. My reviews were in good standing, and I had always received good reports from the clients and visitors. I thought that the timing worked out well.

A few years back I had met Jasmine when she walked in to request an application for employment. The company allowed me the right to use discretion when giving out the applications to the applicants. First of all, I was delighted to see a sister because where I lived and worked there weren't that many. I politely took her application, and I told her the usual script: "We'll keep your application on file. And should something become available within ninety days, we'll be glad to give you a call." I looked over her information and checked for a phone number. After she left, I wrote down her phone number and turned in the application. I kept her numbers for future purposes in case something came up.

Six months later a general office clerk position became available, and I thought about Jasmine. I immediately gave her a call to ask her if she was still searching for a job. She said "yes," and we had a brief conversation. I tried to explain to her my role in all of this, but I couldn't go into detail. I felt that the Lord had put it on my heart to call her, and I obeyed. We both prayed and got our stories together on how we knew each other—from church, we agreed. This was the best way to explain our acquaintance. I asked her if she believed in God, and she said "yes." Then we shared our beliefs about Jesus Christ. I said, "You're no stranger after all."

She didn't get the position. But because the Lord was working things out, another position was created for her. There were times when Jasmine had car trouble, and I let her use mine. She had to perform her job duties in two buildings that were about a fourth of a mile apart. At first it was a little lonely working there and being the only African American woman, but I got used to it.

I was surprised that I didn't get the interview for the job opening; my application was denied. I felt disappointed that H.R. didn't at least have the decency to inform me. At that point I realized that I was only a token that sat at the front desk. I requested to know the reason why my application had been denied. H.R. expressed that I didn't have any MS Office experience. So I started seeking opportunities to take classes to gain the right to dispute any future opportunities if this incident should ever occur again. Eventually I received the basic training of MS Office. I noticed that in the past, I had received a low score on my review because I hadn't had the PC training that I should have completed. Somehow I got penalized for it, plus I had an ancient computer that still operated with DOS.

Desperate to find solutions to the madness, I finally woke up and realized that the years were rolling by. And I wasn't advancing in the direction of being a valuable asset in the job market. In addition to that understanding, I was facing the fact that the company started hiring all these white girls fresh out of college to be administrative assistants. They were purposely overlooking me. Their initiative was to have all the administrative assistants rotate to relieve for my breaks and lunch. When it became time to relieve me, they would either come late or start complaining. I started documenting their unprofessional behavior. My new bosses were talking down to me and being nasty as well. Whenever I called in sick, they would dispute paying for my sick time. Things got very stressful, and I started taking these issues home. I typed memos to the boss explaining the problems I was having. We would have department meetings. And when I would bring up the facts and elaborate on how the other receptionists didn't have to comply by the same rules, the conversation would be dismissed. I was angry and frustrated. But after I got enough documentation on the situation, I figured that I should take it higher.

Saul got tired of me talking about this job because it was giving me the blues. He felt that I should quit and find another job. I wanted to, but something inside wouldn't allow me to walk away. I was tired of the games and the politics. I felt like they were punishing me for having a baby. I submitted a letter to the senior vice president of the company expressing my concerns and issues, and I asked her to intervene. But she wouldn't get involved, and she pushed it back on management. She would, however, politely speak to me and greet me as though I was appreciated.

There was an injustice happening, and I felt compelled to act. I decided to take it a bit further to the EEOC. My whole point was to prove that the company was enforcing certain rules with their African American receptionist that didn't apply to their white receptionist. I was being denied my washroom breaks, and the company condoned such behavior. During my review my boss presented a timer to clock my fifteen-minute breaks. I signed the review despite knowing that things weren't right. It was a trap to set me up to fail, and of course, it set the tone for racial discrimination.

Times like these have caused me to never forget the struggle that took place two hundred years ago when African Americans were emancipated. The EEOC accepted my complaint and expressed that they would be contacting my employer within ninety days. Meanwhile I continued to take the abuse, but I kept praying to God for relief and equality. I wanted to contact the O.T.V. show (*Opinion to Voice*) or NAR (*Need a Resolution*) to expose them, but I didn't have the courage because I figured my story was too small. However, I did contact a brother who had written and published a book on discrimination. His manual was helpful in assisting me in not accepting being treated unfairly.

As the days went by I began to prepare mentally to handle the next step. The best defense supporting my case was my documents and Jasmine. I wanted to quit so many times before I went to the EEOC, but I kept searching for a resolution. The day finally came when management received the letter stating the charge. I was called into a little conference room where I sat at the table with all three devils causing my grief. Their faces were red while they each took a turn to speak. Then I began to express that I wasn't being treated fairly. Immediately they yelled and screamed at me to drop the charges, and they repeated it again, "Drop the charges!" They wanted to intimidate me, but I refused to open my mouth at that point. It was nearly five o'clock. I got up and walked out of the room. I was terrified as I held back tears. When I logged off my computer and reached for my things, I felt rage! I was trembling and shaking all the way home. My nerves were so bad that I started calling on the name of Jesus. When I got inside the house, I was crying, trying to tell Saul about my day. I then reached my decision to resign.

I returned to work the next day to give my letter of resignation. Management knew I wasn't playing. I concluded that I couldn't work in an environment that was causing me this kind of distress. During the last two weeks no one complained, and the atmosphere was pleasant. The senior vice president arranged a meeting with me, and I explained to her that I was not going to tolerate being mistreated and denied a fair opportunity to advance. She didn't consider any of my concerns; her motive was only to coerce me to drop the charges. But I wasn't about to relent. It had been entrapment from the time I returned to work from maternity leave. For the remainder of time I was treated with respect as though nothing had ever happened. The kicker to the story was that management offered to take me out to lunch. I was frightened to accept after the outburst attack, but I agreed to go. I went in the name of Jesus, and I sat in the presence of my enemies, wondering if there was an underlying motive. The conversation was about boring stuff in the news, and they asked me about my new baby. I can honestly say that working there in the last two weeks were the best two weeks since my first two years.

In writing this story and looking back over my life, I think of the scripture in the Bible that says, *God will make your enemies your footstool*. Never in my wildest dreams would I have ever imagined sitting at the table in the presence of my enemies as the outcome. God's words are solid as a rock!

While being consumed with the fight for justice, I had no idea about what I was going to do for income. I had to trust God at that point. I applied for unemployment and was assigned an adjudicator to investigate my reason for leaving my employer. I provided copies of my evidence to support my reason for quitting. I revealed the fact that I had tried to resolve the matter, but due to working under duress, I had been unable to. Once again, God answered my prayers. I was approved for my benefits.

# CHAPTER 8

The summer of 1995 was steaming hot; and when the wind blew, the breeze felt beautiful. Saul received a letter from the state asking him to appear in court regarding baby Doe. I prayed to the Lord, "Let Thy will be done." It had been three long years of waiting for that day to come. On June 27th, Saul returned home with the court papers excluding him as the father of the alleged baby Doe. This was good news for us! We felt relieved because we knew that we would never have to hear from Ms. Doe again.

In the meantime, the unemployment was a blessing. I begin to search for better opportunities through the temporary agency, and I came in contact with nicer people. I felt that I had been in bondage because I didn't know that it was a big world out there. I was holding onto something that was holding me back.

I was allowed to work part-time and receive my unemployment benefits as long as I didn't fall into any of the violations of the guidelines. I landed a part-time assignment, and the unemployment office started calling me weekly and leaving automated messages in regards to work that matched my skills. I could either accept or decline.

But in my case—if I didn't accept the interview—it would jeopardize my benefits. In my search I was seeking diversity because I didn't want to end up in a worse situation than the one I had left behind.

I remember accepting one interview that was pre-arranged through the unemployment office. I decided to play the game. I put on a black skirt with a white and peach short-sleeved shirt. I drew eyeliner on my eyebrows and put a stain on my teeth. I wore sandals with the toes out and no pantyhose, and my toenails were chipped. I was a little musty on purpose. I went to the interview walking with a limp and started looking around to get a feel of the atmosphere. Of course there wasn't an African American in sight.

After the interview I could tell that the manager had an interest in hiring me, but she said that she couldn't pay me what I wanted. I immediately knew that I didn't want to work there, especially after realizing that I might be the only African American. Sometimes that can be a good thing. But from my experience, I was certain I wanted to work for a company that believed in diversity. My whole point was that this agency was not going to put me in any kind of job. I was fighting being confined to a switchboard.

The interviews went on throughout the entire time that I received benefits. When the benefits stopped, I received no more assistance in finding employment. I was on my own. I coasted along until I found a temporary job that offered what I wanted. I was on my way to temping as a career, and one might say, "getting my corporate hustle on."

Then I received some disturbing news about my father's health; he had had bypass surgery. Saul and I went to visit him in Alabama. I bought him a robe and a pair of slippers to show my love and concern. He had a smile on his face, and I could tell that he was happy. I told him that I loved him and that he could call me if he needed anything. I never received a call after my visit, though. That's kind of how things went; my father and I never had good communication that developed into dialogue.

The seasons were changing, and a new year had arrived. I moved on to a better paying assignment. I never tripped about being a temp because I had Saul's insurance. And I also felt at peace with temping because I didn't have to be a part of the office politics. But my life at home was still an emotional roller coaster. I was stressed out—nothing new—and overwhelmed by Saul's behavior. The drinking, staying out late, gambling, and getting high caused me grief and shame. I wore a mask every day when I left home.

I was so disgusted that one evening after he had returned home, I told him that I wanted a divorce. He replied if that was what I was pouting about, he'd give it to me. I couldn't stand for him to touch me or to be in the same house with him. Two weeks later he decided to move in with his brother.

I wasn't mentally prepared for any of the struggles that awaited me. First of all, I didn't have a reliable car because Saul had taken the newer one. I was now on my own raising two kids, and I didn't have the confidence to make it alone. But I wanted Saul out of my life because I was fed up.

Before he moved out, he started complaining that he had lost his house keys. So I never got the locks changed. One Friday evening I heard some noises at the front door. It was Saul trying to get in; he had lied about losing his keys. After I opened the door to let him in, he went into the closet to get a steel baseball bat. He was hoping to catch me with a man. I guess he wanted to take his anger and failures out on someone else. I knew that he was curious about my decision to divorce him, since I was naïve and had taken his abuse for many years.

There was another man I had met—someone in whom I could confide about my pain. He, of course, took my side, telling me how I needed to be loved and to let go of the loser. I was hurting badly, and I wanted to move on, especially with someone who was very interested in me. I didn't feel any reason to feel bad about ending my marriage because it wasn't working.

I proceeded with the divorce, and I received a court date. During the waiting period Saul pursued me for sex, but I refused. So he started saying that I had somebody else. Then, Aunt Vanessa flew into town from California. She had planned to visit for a few days and then leave for Michigan. And she needed a favor from Saul, which put me in the middle. I didn't like where this was leading; but he said that if I rode along, he'd take her. After we rode together listening to love songs in the car and talking on the way back, we ended up in bed together.

Simultaneously my strength left, and my old state of mind returned. I fell back into the bondage of my old feelings of defeat. I felt horrible about my decision to sleep with Saul, and I was haunted by all the old memories of abuse and pain. My spirit became weaker the more I tried to escape from the pit. My thoughts were distorted, and I started thinking negatively about myself.

After I reneged on the divorce, Saul started dragging his feet about when he was coming back. He certainly came back with a cocky and arrogant attitude, throwing his weight around with his chest out as though he was doing me a favor. Before we had sex, now the shoe was on the other foot. But I lost all my strength to break free from this dysfunctional marriage.

We agreed to move out of our apartment and into a new one. Saul felt that we needed a new start, but the real problem was our marriage. It wasn't healthy, nor was it getting any better. He had realized that if I took him back he wouldn't have to pay child support. There's that old saying: *It's cheaper to keep her*. I had a glimmer of hope that maybe we both had learned how to treat one another, but I learned the hard way.

Saul brought debt and additional problems into my life, and the list goes on. Not only did he trail back with new baggage, he dragged several demons along. He wasn't changed at all; he had only become worse. I warned him that if we should ever break up again, there was no coming back. During the short period of time I had spent without him I had felt at peace. Now, when I look back and wonder why I couldn't move forward, it was partly the childcare. It played a big factor in determining my decision to leave or stay with him. I feared not being able to financially handle living on my own.

As I reminisced about the time when we were separated, I realized I hadn't had to worry about what time he was going or coming. I hadn't had to smell any alcohol breath. Finally I suggested that we needed counseling, and I was able to persuade him. We met with a Christian couple, but after a few sessions Saul got discouraged because he felt like his views were being attacked. As he put it, my opinions were always moral. It became a game in his eyes. I was scoring or winning because he was in denial about his actions. The couple insisted that we join their church if we wanted to continue counseling. Saul was not willing to go that far, so they suggested that we seek another church for counseling. Saul wanted to be a part of a bigger church where there was good gospel singing. He suggested his cousin's church in Waukegan. I asked him if we could commit to traveling the distance every Sunday, but he assured me we could.

After joining the church, things were calm for a while—until Saul started making up excuses about why he couldn't attend. When he did go, he'd get high on the way there. I saw marijuana joints in the ashtray. I had never realized that he was an addict until I saw how he had to get high first in order to have a good time or to enjoy normal things. Having a joint was a part of his daily regimen.

His other alibi for missing church was that he was working two jobs to put us into a home. So I had to get the kids ready for church, and we would go without him. I tried to reason with him about not coming, especially since while we were at church he would only be at home in bed getting high. He had me thinking that he was burned out from worrying about making things better. Instead, his addiction was getting worse. I threatened to tell the pastor that he was getting high everyday. He didn't appreciate my threat; so he stated that if I did, he would stop going altogether. I felt bad. It wasn't going to make my marriage any better by exposing his addiction. I was going for my own soul, but I thought Saul wanted to change. I needed God to help me understand my life and to change me.

My responsibilities became heavier; it felt like I was taking care of three babies. All Saul wanted to do was work to get high and buy a new car. That's as far as his mind would allow him to go. When we inquired about buying a home, it was only talk. He was selfish and greedy; and he made up excuses like why the house we would pick wasn't the right one, or the timing was wrong. He would always speak about time as though the years were standing still. He was lost. I began to see that we were on a seesaw: up and down we would go. I struggled again to convince myself that I had to get out of this relationship. I was afraid of growing old and gray listening to his opinions. I knew that we could have been where we wanted to be if he hadn't been an addict.

I dug another type of hole by socializing with too many females. I attracted and maintained superficial friendships because I was miserable. Alexius was the next-door neighbor who had greeted me when we lived at Harmony Villas. Over the course of time her son and J.R. became good playmates. Our sons stayed in touch with each other, and Alexius and I had an off-and-on kind of friendship. Whenever she would get mad at the world, and things weren't going well in her life; she would move away. I could tell that Saul had mixed feelings about her. During the times she was separated from her husband, she would hang around us. She was also an abused woman wearing a mask. She confided in me about her troubled marriage, and she painted a picture of her husband being the bad guy. She told me these sad stories to gain my sympathy, and it worked. I felt compassion for her and her son to the point that I wanted to be there for them. Her family didn't seem supportive, but they were involved from a distance.

Alexius was a closet-needy person. I offered her help with job leads as I knew how to get my corporate hustle on. But in my spirit I never felt completely comfortable about her because there was something about her that seemed phony. I became uncomfortable and suspicious whenever she would blow steam about not coming over to visit if Saul was going to be home. I had detected a mutual vibe from the both of them. He would say things to demean or prejudge her character. He said that she could be a dyke since she wanted to hang around me so much. I never picked that up in her spirit, but I did feel that she was envious sometimes. I didn't know whether it was harmful, though. We continued to move past it.

Sometimes I noticed when I would be at home spending time with my family, she would show up or call to talk. If Saul was home, he would get uncomfortable after I told him it was Alexius on the phone or at the door. Instead of telling me what was really on his mind or being discreet about the matter, he would leave to allow us to talk.

One morning I woke up mad from having a dream about her and Saul. My intuition was trying to tell me something. I dialed her number around seven a.m. to ask her if she was sleeping with my husband. She denied it, and she became upset with me for asking. Then she immediately wanted to know what he had said. She confessed that she had met him outside at the trash dumpster at our old apartment. He was driving by and had stopped to ask her some questions. But at the time her husband was watching from the patio. Then she changed the subject, telling me she had encountered this same issue with other women being jealous of her because of their men. I suspected the reason why she was being confronted by that kind of scenario was because she had a lustful spirit and acted like a tomboy. As time went on, she backed away from us. I prayed that God would handle that situation and put my thoughts on positive things. I had reached the decision to go back to school to further my education at the community college.

Violet, Aunt Vanessa's oldest daughter and a young mother as well, came to town to visit for a week. A month later I received a phone call from Aunt Vanessa. She was pleasant at first, and then her attitude became hostile when she expressed her reason for calling. She was furious and angry at Saul. She gave me the news that he had made a sexual advance towards Violet. I immediately felt disgusted and sick to my stomach. While I was listening to Vanessa, I stared at Saul with rage filling my heart. After that phone call, I sat back to rewind my thoughts. I remembered coming home one evening after work and feeling strange. Violet had been sitting on the living room sofa watching TV, and J.R. was downstairs visiting a friend. Saul was in the kitchen cooking tacos for dinner, and I noticed that he was high. Violet asked if I could make sure that no one came into the bathroom while she took her shower. I said, "Of course," but an eerie feeling had crept inside my spirit. The whole incident put a wedge between my Aunt Vanessa and me. She suggested that I leave Saul. I was sick and embarrassed because I felt ashamed.

One morning while taking a shower I noticed some bleeding. I examined myself, but I didn't see any cuts after I got out of the shower. After I dried off, the bleeding re-appeared. But this time I detected that it was coming from my breast. I panicked, and I called a friend to ask what was happening. She suggested that I go to the hospital. At the time I had X-rays taken, but I had to wait for the test results to come back. It was September 12th. While I was sitting in the waiting room at the hospital for my results, I started to feel nauseous. I tried to ignore it, but the feeling persisted. All of a sudden my ears started popping, and I couldn't hear. As it progressed I felt the urge to defecate. I asked the woman sitting next to me if she would watch my things. Then I slowly got up to search for the washroom. While I was walking my sight became blurry. I panicked as I leaned on the walls to find my way. When I found the washroom door, I started to recite the Twenty-Third Psalm. The woman coming out stopped to ask if I was okay, but I didn't answer. I was struggling to stay conscious while I prayed. I made it into the stall to sit down, and less than two seconds later a heavyset woman with a loud voice said, "Wake up, honey." She opened my stall to wet my face with paper towels. By her presence, I knew that God was on my side. There was a man waiting with a wheelchair when she pulled me off the toilet. I was taken into a patient room to lie down. Then a nurse came to give me a check-up and evaluate my condition. She felt that I might have been overwhelmed by the anticipation of my test results, but she assured me that there were no findings of anything to worry about. The whole experience was very frightening. Coming that close to losing my vision and hearing, I had assumed that I was dying. It was one of the scariest moments in my life.

After that experience, I wrote my godsister Amaris a letter. We had lost contact with each other after I moved. I was concerned about how she was doing because she had cancer. When I had last talked to her a year ago, it was in remission. We stopped talking because she felt I was not spending enough time with her. She would tell me that the people I thought were my friends weren't my true friends. I respected her opinion, but I didn't agree. I had my own set of problems, and I felt it best to distance myself to keep the peace. I slowly drifted away, and I realized that life does that to certain friendships. After Amaris got sick, there was a change in her spirit because everything became competitive. I had never wanted things to ever get so bad between us that we couldn't speak. I understood the health issue, but when I talked to her she acted like life was going well. But I knew the truth because she wore a mask, too.

I felt that my life and marriage were the worse among my peers, but over time I found out that she had married an addict, too. We both were married to functioning addicts who went to work faithfully. We camouflaged our lives to the world. It had me at the brink of losing my mind and soul. It costs a lot to love a person on drugs because you become consumed with masking lies. You lose yourself in the process of living.

On September 15, 1997, I received a call from an acquaintance to inform me that Amaris had died on September 12th. I felt devastated. I sat around all day to reminisce about our times together, wondering if she had ever received my card. The day of her death was the same day I had my unforgettable experience at the hospital. When I got in touch with her family, I wanted to know if she had received my card; but she hadn't because her family had moved. I was deeply sad because I had written in my letter that I wanted to express forgiveness and make amends. It was my way of letting her know that I was maturing. And no matter what I would always be her friend.

I attended her funeral and hung around the family. Her little nieces, who had grown up, told me that she would say things like, "I wonder what Naima is doing." When I heard that, it evoked deep emotions inside my soul. Sometimes words aren't enough when you're dealing with a life or death experience. I realized that I had tried to reach her before it was too late. I had respected Amaris' illness by visiting as often as she would allow. Since seeing several people that I was close to get cancer, I had noticed that they tended to act strangely as the disease progressed. One particular behavior that I didn't understand was turning mean and going into hiding. I didn't know how to process losing someone that I was close to this way. It was a wake-up call to start keeping up with my mammograms. I thought that it was ironic I had a near death experience on the same day that she died, and I had to know the time that she passed away. It was at nighttime in the tenth hour, and my event had taken place during the tenth hour that a.m. I was spooked by this because I knew that she had been very unhappy about our friendship. I had to forgive myself for not being able to be there and put the rest in God's hands.

## CHAPTER 9

School was back in session. I had never thought I would go to college, but I had successfully made it through the first semester with a 4.0 GPA. I started my second semester classes, but I lost focus and slacked on my homework. Since I was falling behind, I decided to drop out. I couldn't balance all the demands that came with having kids and a husband, so I started putting that time into my kids and staying close to home. I was tense all the time, though, because I had to be five people every day: wife, mother, employee, maid, and myself. Honestly, it was difficult to persevere through all my challenges and adversities.

When the New Year came, I wanted to make a change. And for my resolution, I decided to simplify my life. I searched to find things that would give me that positive push. I started with positive thinking. I had to tell myself that no matter how hard things seemed, I couldn't repeat attempting suicide. This time I knew better, and I had enough time to contemplate my situation. I found that reading inspirational and self-help books and listening to smooth jazz and gospel gave me the positive outlook I needed. I practiced my computer skills, exercised, and went for long walks while I talked to God. My role got difficult as I matured—or should I say, as I persevered to fight for a better life. I accepted a permanent job, thinking it was time to settle down. But between the job and my marriage, I got very ill.

I had been hired as an administrative assistant; but during the first month, the company fired their receptionist. I was trapped again as a receptionist even though the company tried to hire temps. My workday was unpredictable. I was floating from my desk to the switchboard. Wherever I was needed, that's where I worked for the day or week.

The majority of my time was spent at the switchboard. My boss was trying to micromanage my time. He seemed fair at first, but he became territorial. I was his administrative assistant, but not exclusively. What he wanted wasn't going to happen; the nature of the job was to assist the other departments with various projects and relieve the receptionist. He took his frustrations out on me. Instead of having the balls to address the switchboard matter to Human Resources, he therefore took the path of looking at my weaknesses to displace his frustrations.

More issues started to arise, and again it was memo time. My boss refused to identify that the switchboard position was tied into my administrative duties. I couldn't get him to prioritize my work. And during my three-month review, he focused on what my weaknesses were along with goals that weren't attainable. I didn't agree with his expectations, so I decided to take it to H.R

In the meantime, I went along with the game. Eventually the company hired a receptionist, and I attended EAP for counseling to search for answers as to why I kept attracting this type of work in my job search. But the stress from work took a toll on my health. One morning I woke with numbness and tingling in my hands, legs, and feet. This progressed into other things. I started urinating up to eight times a night. I was worrying profusely about going to work and sitting at the switchboard. I learned that I was having panic attacks. When I talked, my breathing would get short. My body was tense and stressed as though it had a mind of its own. Everything that I was going through became internal, which caused my body to react. I was holding my emotions and pain inside by trying to suppress them. I exercised on my lunch hour in hopes that I could get a handle on things. I had access to use the corporate health spa and the other facilities on campus. The job had some awesome benefits, which is why I didn't want to quit.

On one particular Friday, which happened to be Good Friday, I was walking around the lake with Saul when all of sudden I couldn't walk. My legs had stopped, and I panicked. I forced one leg in front of the other. At that point I knew that I needed intervention, and some changes had to take place in my life. I started mentally fighting back by asking for prayer, and I searched for a good doctor.

My sister-in-law recommended that I buy some virgin olive oil and pray over it with the Twenty-third

Psalm. Then I should anoint my body from head to toe every morning. I immediately followed her advice, and I kept the faith that God was going to heal me. I also started seeing all kinds of specialists and having X-rays. All of my tests results were diagnosed as normal—although my symptoms were getting worse. I was losing hope day by day, until a lady from my job recommended a doctor who believed in holistic healing. She was a Godsend. The doctor recommended that I find another job, and she recommended for me to get counseling for my marriage. I begin taking the herbs she prescribed, and I received physical therapy.

The day I started taking the herbs I felt instant results. I took a walk around the lake while praising God for answering my prayers. I went from blowing into a brown paper bag when I hyperventilated to being able to breathe one breath at a time. I went on vacation with my family.

When I returned to work, the receptionist quit. I had seen it coming, and I realized what the job was doing to my health. So I left work on medical leave for two weeks, and my symptoms improved. Then I resigned from the job, knowing it was a medical decision. I was blessed again to receive my unemployment benefits.

The years were passing by, and fall of 1999 was the year my baby started kindergarten. I was able to put him on the school bus and be home when the bus dropped him off. Of course, I couldn't kick back because the unemployment office had started calling for employment opportunities. I went on the interviews, but I was trying to stay away from receptionist work. Obviously my receptionist experience stood out as a strong attribute that most employers recognized as an asset. But I had gained computer skills as well as organizational skills. I updated my resume to reflect my strengths and the duties that I wanted to perform. I got frustrated, but I kept going. God was showing me that the doors that were shut were not the places He wanted me to be. He allowed me to see it for myself, as I went on the interviews. I became wiser in discerning if I was going to have problems down the road with a particular company. All was well with my soul when I didn't get hired. I had faith to believe that I was more than just a receptionist, and I wasn't going to let anybody turn me around.

On the day of an interview, I would look in the mirror at myself. I saw an ambitious, determined African American woman who was favored and blessed. It didn't matter about the outcome because I knew God was with me. One particular company showed an interested in me, but they didn't want to pay me what I asked for. And they weren't willing to negotiate. So I kept searching.

A month later I was again offered a position with less pay, and again I declined. I felt good, boosting my confidence that I was marketable and qualified. I believed that one day I would get what I prayed for. I started analyzing the vicinity of my job search because I believed that it contributed to some of the unwanted problems that I was encountering. I decided to search in a different location that offered a diversified work community. I signed up with a new temporary agency in the area, and I got a short-term assignment in January of 2000. While I was on the assignment, an employee presented me with an opportunity. I was able to find out about the work atmosphere. I had an exploratory interview with the manager. He came across doubting that I could successfully perform the job to his expectations. He was a brother who had a lustful spirit and a chip on his shoulder. I knew right away from the looks of it to keep temping.

As I pondered these thoughts—"*keep looking underneath every rock, because I will find what I'm looking for*"—I bought the Sunday paper and saw an ad for World USA. They were looking for a technical person. I liked their benefits, so I faxed over my resume. I got a call from H.R. to interview for an administrative assistant position. It was a panel interview where I had to be alert to answer questions about my schooling. Once again, they were concerned about my personal goals. The position didn't require a degree, but of course my lack of a degree was another reason to disqualify me. I had to cut it short because I sensed where things were heading.

My current assignment was ending, and I still hadn't secured anything. Then I received a call from the temp service to temp at World USA. I accepted the assignment and begin temping in the position that I had been denied. I went along with everything as though I had never been there.

One day the boss needed some urgent help with a PowerPoint presentation, and the other administrative assistant didn't know PowerPoint. I offered what I knew, and I handled the situation. A few days later I was offered the job permanently, but I declined. The job wasn't challenging. In addition to that, the other administrative assistant wanted to micromanage my time.

During this time my marriage was over in my mind. My emotions and thoughts were not in harmony. Whenever I reflected on my marriage and analyzed my future with Saul, my mind only thought the worst. And the disconnection weighed on me. I settled with the fact that I could always look back and say that at least I tried to fight for my marriage. Saul was doing stupid stuff he could no longer hide. He left the car keys in the ignition, and he also left rolled up joints on the car seat. There was money and bags of marijuana in the trunk. That was his hiding place where he stashed away his devilment. I sat him down and asked him what the hell was going on. He told me that he was working too many hours, but he couldn't tell me why. His company's stock plan was doing well on NASDAQ. He had a nice amount of shares invested with his company, and things were looking really good on the financial side. We were truly blessed, but our marriage existed only because I couldn't see my way out. I felt as though I was talking to a zombie when I looked into his eyes.

One night while I was sleeping, I began fighting a demon that was pulling my husband away from me at the foot of our bed. I was screaming to the top of my lungs, "Satan, the blood of Jesus is against you!" and Saul woke me up. I could actually hear myself repeating the words as he shook me. Around five days later he made a confession that he was hooked on crack cocaine. I started crying uncontrollably because I knew that he was changing, and his ways were scaring me. His memory was getting worse, and he couldn't cope with a bad day without getting high. I felt an instant death between us. I went through the phase of trying to fix the matter through praying with him and taking over the finances. I asked him to get some intervention. I asked him to tell his brother, whom he admired, because I couldn't deal with all this alone. This problem was bigger than a secret, and it was fatal to my sanity. My mother had always told me to keep some insurance on Saul, because a fool will hang himself. Saul was one of those people who didn't believe that fat meat was greasy. He never feared anything, which sometimes could be a good thing, but it could also be bad. Saul was a loose cannon and out of control.

I tried to digest the news that he had progressed to this next phase of drugs. I asked myself, *What's next—losing his job, dope dealing, and endangering our lives?* He had gotten several DUIs, and he had even gotten shot at in our car while driving down an alley in Chicago. I stayed on my knees in prayer with God to keep him alive and to deliver me from this madness. This was my wake-up call. I didn't want to be with Saul anymore; he was losing his mind. I felt that this was a personal choice to choose drugs. It wasn't a natural tragedy; it was a self imposed one.

My thoughts ran around in circles as I panicked about the future and where I would end up if I stayed with him. He was regressing due to the drugs, and his morals were all screwed up. It hurt more that I had to let go of our plans of growing old together with our kids and grandchildren. Then I started feeling guilty about bailing out because we had so many years of struggles together. Our Southern roots ran deep in terms of "being down" for each other. So I vowed to stand by his side and give him a fair chance at combating his addiction. The next step was intervention, which of course was his choice to get counseling or attend a rehab program. Saul was dragging his feet on this issue. So I gave him an ultimatum: get some help, or else I was going to throw in the towel. He tried to convince me that with a few sessions of counseling, he would be a new person. First of all, however, he didn't want to pay for it. In his eyes he saw that money as being a waste. That was the conclusion to the outpatient counseling.

One day he came home from work to ask me if I would cosign to get a loan from a finance company. His finances were out of control. He was bouncing checks, and people were calling the house. In the past every time his money had gotten off track, he would want me to fix it. I would put our money into the same account and work a budget until things got better. As soon as it got straightened out, he would act a fool and demand his money back so he could do it again. I lost this battle every time.

We got into an altercation because I wouldn't agree to sign for the loan. He went into my purse, and he saw a sheet of paper with some writing on it saying, "I love you, cuz." He demanded that I explain it to him. I started explaining to him that it was a fax document I had sent to Paris to help her confirm that her fax machine was working. I tried to say all that in one breath, but before I could finish he struck me in the eye with his fist. He continued to hit me until I fell to the floor. I screamed, and I begged Jacob, my youngest son, to come into the bedroom, thinking it would cause Saul to come to his senses. He finally did after I yelled at him that I could prove the fax was innocent. I got up and dialed the number from the living room phone where Jacob was sitting on the couch, watching cartoons. While Saul was talking, I ran out the house to find a pay phone to call the police. I was crying, devastated, and I knew that Saul was on drugs and going crazy.

After I made it to the pay phone, I called Paris collect. She clicked me in to say that she was on the other line talking to Saul. She was trying to read the paper to him that I had faxed to her. I told her what he'd done to me, and that I was going to call the police on him. But she convinced me to give him another chance. I could hear these words resonate in the back of my mind. In the past he had made the threat, "If I ever call the police he'd beat my ass." The next thing I knew he was circling the parking lot at the store where I was. He asked me to get in the car to come home. At this time I knew that J.R. was still at school. I was startled, but I agreed because Jacob was home alone.



The next day I had severe eye pain, and I couldn't stand the sunlight. The pain got worse, and the only relief I had was when I closed all of the curtains. I had to eventually go to the E.R. The pain was excruciating when any sunlight shone on my eye to the point that I had to wear shades. The doctors demanded that I explain what happened, but I made up a lie.

During this time Saul's cousin died, and we went to pay our respects to the family. I felt silly sitting at the funeral wearing shades. I guess Saul felt sorry because he decided to tell his job that he had a drug problem. But they didn't believe him because he was very skilled at his job, and he was able to do triple scale of what they wanted. He tried admitting himself over the phone to the hospital, but they wouldn't accept him. He came home stating that he had tried but no one had taken him seriously. I told him that he was in bad shape, and that there was no way I was going to settle until he got some help. I told him to put on his worst clothes and put his shirt on backwards with the tag out and his dirty gym shoes. I made him look like a bum so the hospital could look at his outward appearance and make an informed decision. I drove him to the hospital, and they admitted him. I was relieved because I could tell that he didn't want to stay.

We were fine financially at this time, as he had liquidated some shares to tide things over. Saul treated this time as a vacation, but it was a living nightmare for me. I had the temp agency place me on the inactive list for a while. My life was an extreme mess, and my mind was distorted. Saul was in rehab for fourteen days before being released for outpatient counseling. When he got home he acted like a new man. I mean, there was no drinking or drugging; he talked about the Big Book and the Twelve Steps. I stayed on edge, monitoring his behavior and progress. I paid close attention to how he was reacting to the things he used to do. His attitude about his money was different, but I could tell that he felt powerless. He was acting very calm and talking right for the first forty days and attending his outpatient meetings. I had never seen such a positive change in my relationship since our first two years of being married. We did the family thing together, taking walks, riding bikes, and cooking together. It was a beautiful experience because he was clean and sober.

It didn't last very long, however. He started getting antsy, and I could tell that he was restless. He found reasons to complain while he was lying around the house. He became defiant and reversed the roles making accusations that I was on drugs. I had my own hobbies, and I had become accustomed to him not being there to occupy that space. The kids had each other, and he felt like his new life was the pits. Therefore, he relapsed, and that was the end of his sobriety.

I surrendered. I went back to work for the agency, who sent me back to World USA. I asked them to put me on a short-term assignment due to the fact that I was contemplating relocation. I was at World USA for two weeks when my boss offered me the job, but I declined. I politely told him that I would be glad to train the new person or the next temp. He came back a week later to ask if I would reconsider my decision. I didn't want to appear ungrateful, so I told him that I needed to discuss it further with my husband. I was so confused about my life; I didn't know which way to go. Finally I accepted the offer.

I started counseling sessions to help me face reality and to vent. I was psychologically unable to make any healthy decisions about how to leave my marriage. I felt that I was buried so deeply that my eyes were open, but I was walking dead. I kept praying to God to change my life if He didn't change my husband.

Alexius's son called J.R. to inform him that they were back in town. Our sons started talking on the phone again, and that's when she and I started up our dialogue again. I was very vulnerable, and of course, I started telling her how I was doing. She couldn't believe that I had been hired to work for World USA. She was looking for employment, too, and she wanted my help. Each prospect that I had previously recommended to her for employment had hired her. She was currently temping at the assignment where I had previously temped. She wanted to get hired on at World USA, and I told her that anything was possible because there was nothing that God couldn't do if you believed. I got her an application. And before we knew it, she was hired as a permanent employee. We both worked on the same floor under the same director.

It turned out Alexius was low on money, and she had no place to live. In the past I had loaned her money for gas in between paydays—you know, the stuff you do for a person that you feel is your friend. This time she needed big money, so I drew up a contract between us. She didn't want to sign it, and she acted as if she had a problem with it. But I made it clear to her that no contract meant no money. I told her that if she had true intentions of paying me back, she wouldn't hesitate to sign. Then her car quit on her, and I gave her one of ours that was on its last legs. In the process of helping her, I was telling her bit-by-bit all my business. I was too confused and in a state of distress to care. She pretended to be my friend, and I fell into her trap of lies and manipulation.

During the summer of 2000, I went to Michigan for a week. And out of fun, I went to see a psychic. The psychic said that there was a woman at my job who was jealous of me. The psychic also told me that I was going to leave my husband. I knew that I was well on my way to finding the strength.

As time went on, I started saving my money. I didn't know how or when it was going to happen, but I stayed in counseling and continued to pray. I needed to stay connected to some spiritual help, so I would visit different churches that my friends attended. Saul was completely back to his old ways, and he was trying to pick fights because he didn't want to feel guilty about using. When his eyes were red and glossy, I knew what time it was. I became so disgusted around him; I had lost respect for him. He tried to threaten me when I didn't want to have sex by going through my purse. He wanted to intimidate me like before and have a reason to start punching on me. I never backed down from a fight, but I knew that I wasn't fighting a sane person. I was living in fear, and I wanted to find shelter and peace.



During Thanksgiving, my family from Michigan decided to visit. While they were in town, I started my apartment search because our lease was about to expire. And I knew that I wasn't going to renew it. I was approved for a two-bedroom apartment, and I put down a deposit to hold the apartment for my move-in date. When I returned home, I assessed the atmosphere before breaking the news to Saul. He was sitting in the bathtub singing and getting high when I announced that I was leaving. I braced myself because I was afraid of his reaction. He looked at me and said, "That's fine." At that point I knew there was no turning back.

On January 5, 2001, I moved into my very first apartment without my husband. I remember being afraid of living on my own. I had doubts that I could afford to pay the rent. I was hoping to take both of my sons, but Saul held J.R. against my will. He warned me to stop telling J.R. that he was moving. I was walking on eggshells, and anything Saul said caused me to cry. I felt like a wimp in many ways, mainly because I didn't have the strength to fight dirty. After that moment, I kept my mouth shut. I believe that it was in God's plan to allow me to leave without being harmed. J.R. was fifteen, and he was Saul's sole support. Saul wasn't letting him go.

While unpacking my items, I paused to exhale. I couldn't believe that I had finally gotten out safe and alive. I felt relieved at not having to smell cigarettes and liquor breath. Jacob was very sad because he didn't understand why we had to split up the family. He wondered why J.R. wasn't coming with us. I tried to explain things to him the best way that I could. I wasn't good at dealing with my issues or expressing what I needed to say to make sense of everything. I remember crying a lot of tears at night and sometimes at work. The emotional pain was stabbing me like a knife right in the heart.

My greatest fear was facing failure if I didn't make it on my own. Things didn't seem right being a single parent. I struggled emotionally about having to do it, but it wasn't the end of the world. I had never looked down on other single parents, but it was devastating to become a statistic. I wanted to make the transition as comfortable for Jacob as possible by allowing him to remain in his school, so I sacrificed by driving every day ten extra miles. My plate was full with the job, a separation, and new responsibilities.

After Alexius finished paying back the loan, she quit work. She had complained about her life and the job the whole time. I recall telling her that I had moved adjacent to her apartment. She offered to help with moving if I needed any assistance. I took her up on her offer to have Jacob's bedroom set picked up and delivered by U-Haul, and she volunteered her brother's help as long as I paid him. I accepted their offer because I didn't have anyone else.

Alexius was acting strangely towards me, but this wasn't new. I ignored her, and I amused myself decorating my new place. She assisted me with lifting the heavy furniture and assembling whatever I needed. Once I got settled in, I felt certain that I needed to start the divorce. I barely received any financial support for Jacob because Saul was bitter that I wouldn't sleep with him. I proceeded with the divorce, and he pretended to cooperate by signing all the papers—except for one. I wanted to forge his signature, something you learn how to do when you're married. But for some reason, I didn't do it. Still, thinking back on how much suffering he caused me, I wished that I had.

Saul decided to disagree with us settling things on our own. He made it very difficult for me. I knew at this point that I needed to start fighting back. I hired an attorney, who gave me an estimate of what the fees would cost for the divorce. And he drew up a payment plan.

The first three months of being on my own were the hardest; it was lonely coming home to an empty place. I had a lot of free time on my hands. I started finding events to attend with my friends. Shay was an acquaintance that I had met on one of my temporary assignments. We made a connection through some similar life experiences, and we remained in touch. As time went on, we became closer through some family dinners. One weekend Shay decided to visit. We had a conversation about men, and she said that she knew a nice bachelor. I asked what was wrong with him, if he was a God fearing man, what he looked like, and whether he was into drinking and drugs. Well, of course, she said all the right answers. She went on to tell me about how she knew him through her brother. Her brother and this Mr. Prospect grew up together. I was hesitant about dating anyone because I knew that it was too soon. I wasn't even divorced on paper yet. But in my heart, I knew I wasn't going back to Saul. I had learned what mistakes not to make. I knew I was dealing with another spirit. I understood what type, too, and being unequally yoked with another soul wasn't an easy thing to break free from.

I felt that I was starting all over, and so it wouldn't hurt to meet a new friend. Shay and I arranged to meet Koz and her brother at Chili's one evening. When I laid eyes on him I couldn't get a good look. I wanted to stare at him to see if I was attracted to him, but I didn't want to be rude or obvious. I wasn't able to pick up anything weird in his spirit other than the fact that he was loud after he warmed up. He had on some jeans with a jersey and a baseball cap. Towards the end of the evening, Koz and I agreed to go on a date. I guess he liked what he saw, but I wasn't wooed. After seeing him for the second time, however, I immediately discovered that I didn't like the way that he dressed. He was attractive in his own way, aside from having a belly. He wore some dingy black jeans with a paisley print shirt. I was turned off by this; my first impression of him was fading fast. Shay had assured me that he could really dress, but obviously that was her opinion. I didn't want to go any further. But after I shared what I felt about meeting him, I listened to some outside advice—a person's heart can be right, and their taste for fashion outdated.

On our third date we were in his neck of the woods. While we were driving, we passed by some apartments where another friend of mine lived. I mentioned it to him while we were passing, just keeping conversation. He gave me a funny look that startled me, so I asked him if he knew who I was referring to. Then he started describing her. I smiled, and he had a grin on his face. I didn't know how to take it until he asked me if her name was Lila. My next question was if he had ever dated her. He said "no," but that he knew her ex-boyfriend.

As soon as I returned home, I called Lila to tell her about Koz. She admitted that she knew him, too. And in addition to that she said I had met him before, around Christmas of 1999 when I stopped over to pick up some gifts. Koz had dropped by to pick up his friend KC. And that was when we were introduced. I was amazed by it, because I do remember the incident. We immediately felt that this had to be fate because Lila and Shay had never met, and they both lived on different sides of the state. It was ironic that Shay had mentioned Koz one time or another in the past while I was over her house visiting.

After we had been seeing each other for about a month, Koz started to become apprehensive about getting close. He didn't know what to think of my situation since Saul and I had been together for half my life. Koz was doing a lot of talking and putting two and two together. He said that he remembered KC talking about one particular weekend when he had met a couple through Lila. I invited Lila and KC over for dinner. KC was a Southerner and fit right in with Saul because they both got drunk. I guess he had a good time, because he went back and told Koz everything. KC and Saul talked the whole time about life and living down South.

Koz was analyzing my life through these instances. He became curious even more to the point that Shay's brother's wife warned him to take it slow. She was giving him advice, but it seemed as though she enjoyed letting it be known that she had some influence over whom he dated. I didn't understand where he was going with this, as I had nothing to hide. But at this point he was fishing for information to determine if he wanted to proceed with a relationship. But I realized that he wanted to keep me in the layaway when he asked if I had a problem with dating him exclusively. I said "no." I was fine about it because he wasn't trying to jump my bones like most guys would have.

Saul was calling frequently to try and persuade me to come back. I just assumed that the bills were pilling up. Since I wasn't talking about coming back, he said that he had found someone to move in. When I asked if I knew this person, he said *kinda sorta*. I wanted to know who she was, but he said that he was going to wait to make sure that it was official. Little did I know that this was his way of softening the blow. I was not ready to see how dirty he could get; he wanted revenge. I suppressed my thoughts about it and rolled with the punches.

One morning I heard the Lord speak. "Why do you feel like you need a man when I am supplying your needs?" I heard these words clearly, but I wasn't paying it any attention. I was concentrating on Koz and trying to figure how to go forward with things on my own. Meanwhile, Koz and I did a lot of talking on the phone, and his bill was getting expensive. We lived over an hour apart, and he complained about the cost of gas that he was spending. I sympathized with him, so we had to find a way to compromise. We had a conversation over the phone one evening, and he became loud and evil because I didn't agree with something he said. My feelings were hurt, and I felt hesitant about whether I should continue seeing him.

My birthday was coming up, and he had talked about buying me something nice. Shay and Lila had schooled me that he treated his girlfriends with the finest. They were right. He bought me a ring for my birthday, and we went to dinner.

The day after my birthday Saul called to break the news that he was sleeping with Alexius. She was the secret that he had been holding out on a few weeks ago. My voice started trembling over the phone as a sharp pain penetrated my heart. It felt like he had gotten a knife and ripped it apart. My eyes started to water, and I told him that I had to get off the phone. He was laughing, saying, "It's like that, you know." I told him that they deserved each other, and that he'd gotten the dirtiest whore out there. And then I hung up the phone. I cried while I leaned over the kitchen sink to hold my balance. I started reminiscing about all the times that I had suspected this! God had been trying to reveal it to me the whole time, but I was too busy to listen. I wanted to injure myself, but instead I made a phone called to distract myself from doing anything stupid. Subsequently I pulled myself together as I started to reminisce that Alexius had resigned after six months of employment, around the second month that I had left Saul. I had seen her at a four-way stop sign near my apartment and blew my horn, but she drove right past me.

My spirit became sad after that because I needed to face the truth about her. My mother had always warned me about having any female friends. When I look back, I can see the evidence of her philosophy to be somehow true. She tried to convert my thinking before she died, but I never took heed. The pain of all this became too overwhelming to hold inside. I started sharing my deepest emotions with Koz because I had no peace. I thought I could handle it on my own, but apparently it was more than I could bear. I wanted to leave my past behind, but there were things that weren't settled. I was hurting, and I needed to be comforted.

On the days that I didn't talk about it, Koz would bring it up. And I could tell that he was throwing it back in my face. It was the highlight of our conversations, and things started to spiral downhill, a new nightmare unfolding. He started calling on his breaks at night to pick arguments, saying mean things, and using profanity a lot. He went into making comparisons about what I had versus what he had. At this point another spirit jumped inside his body and took over. I told him that I had never argued with anyone that much in my entire life.

The divorce was moving slowly because my attorney was after more money. He expressed a strong dislike for Saul, and somehow all that created another nightmare. My lawyer's professional attitude had changed; he took on a nasty disposition. When he addressed my case, the tone in his voice was harsh; and he became impatient. He made it very clear that I had married a fool. In my opinion he wanted to milk me because we both had decent jobs and cars. He asked about Saul's family financial status, digging for information about money. He even expressed that he wasn't going to make any money from my case. I mean, this ordeal became relentless.

At my first court appearance, I thought I was going to receive child support, but that never happened. Saul was acting evil, saying mean and hateful things. He threatened that he was going to fight to get custody of the boys, and he confessed that he had the financial backings to win. He expressed that I could go on with my life and have more babies by my new man. He was operating under a drug spirit. And I wasn't strong enough to ignore his negativity or display the strength that I needed to make him accept the fact that it was over between us. He had screwed up his life, and then he became bitter because I chose not to support his addictions. And I allowed him to punk me around with his manipulative and conning ways. When he was running off at the mouth, he called me "Lexis" in court. I had a flashback when he said that because I remembered when he first gave me a nickname. I started crying because of the insults. He knew what strings to pull to make me cry or give up.

Koz was sitting outside the courtroom waiting. He was trying to listen to hear how things were going. I see now that this was a bad move, because he started venting his anger towards Saul. He became emotionally involved with my trash. I couldn't see how this was affecting him or the price I would have to pay later.

Court didn't go well at all, so we got a continuance, which added more fees to my bill. Saul lied to my attorney by sending him a letter from his lawyer explaining that he was representing him, but this so-called attorney never appeared. Koz was mad because he could see through the games, and he recognized the fact that Saul didn't want to let me go. He was pressuring me to hurry up and detach myself. I was getting flack from Koz and my lawyer. Saul made things difficult for me to become detached, emotionally and on paper. I told Koz that he could keep going if he chose to because it didn't matter which way the wind blew. His motto was that if you could make it through four seasons with him, then you were the one. Over and over again I would listen to his philosophies.

Jasmine called to tell me that she knew a guy who had a prophetic word. I asked her how he knew of me, and she said that he'd described me to another mutual friend. I arranged to meet with him at his church. I wasn't afraid because Jasmine and another mutual friend were there as well. This man stated that God had given him a message: that He was sanctioning a husband for me. I asked him how I would know when I met the person that God had ordained for me. He replied simply that I would just know. I received what he said and prayed about it.

There was an enormous amount of pressure coming from every angle in my life. Koz played the cards of keeping me exclusive and putting everything he wanted to buy me on layaway. He bragged a lot about his car, stocks, the condo, and mainly how he had it going on. His ego was working overtime. He couldn't handle or deal with what I had to go through. I suppose that was why he had to draw some attention to himself. He started telling me that I had too much baggage and drama, and that no man was going to want me. But I just told him that he could get "to stepping." I knew I had to finish what I had started, with or without him.

Obviously what I was saying went in one ear and out the other because he called me real late one night to tell me that I was "bourgie." I admit that I enjoy the finer things in life and I'm conscious about where I want to live. I didn't know where he was going with this because the tone of his voice sounded harsh. I told him that he was verbally abusive and crazy; then he hung up on me. I couldn't see how things had gotten so off track; I had just cooked dinner and baked him a cake. I felt like I was drowning in my sea of misery.

It became apparent that Koz's main problems were insecurity and intimidation. He demeaned my position at my job, and he loved to argue. He was constantly keeping the drama going between us because he had a competitive spirit. We never went to church together. He said that I was still married, and that it wasn't right; but he was lusting after me the whole time. He didn't think it was a sin to "bump and grind." He'd had a bitter breakup with his fiancée, so he was carrying baggage as well. He still had the engagement ring. And his plans were to trade it in and buy me one **if** I made it through the "four seasons."

In August 2001, I met a temp at my job. During our conversations, I found out that she attended the same church where I had gone to meet the prophet. She knew of him as well. I felt that this was another ironic coincidence of a small world. Over a period of time, she revealed that she had met a psychic. This was a psychic, who had given her some solid information in the past, and she convinced me to visit her. I was hesitant about repeating that again, but I decided to go ahead with it since it was only fifteen dollars. The reading that I received was close to the first psychic's reading. She spoke about my future husband, and she also stated that I was born to work for myself through my God-given talents and creativity. Everything, of course, sounded really good. Then she suggested I come to her for cleansing. She said that I needed a spiritual counselor to assist me to get those things. I saw her on two other occasions before I came to my senses. The cleansing was about more money, entangling my soul with that dark world. I repented to God and ended things right away.

Meanwhile Satan was still busy; my lawyer conjured up another plan to ask for money. I had paid him in full for all fees for the petition he had originally drawn up. This made me angry, and I told him that he wasn't going to get another dime. I had paid him more than what the original contract stated, and I still wasn't receiving any child support. He threatened to drop my case, but I knew that he couldn't based on legalities and the amount of time he had spent on it. It was up to me, the client, to fire him—which was his next plan. I told him that I was going to ride it out to the end, and if he couldn't get me divorced—then it would be a pending case. When I said that, his attitude changed. I realized that he wanted to be done with me as much as I wanted this whole nightmare to be over. He came up with another strategy that worked.

It took eight months to divorce that spirit of sorrow that I had loved for years. I came to the conclusion that my lawyer, my ex, and Koz could all watch my smoke. I broke off my relationship with Koz in the "third season," two weeks after my divorce became final. I sent him a text message and a letter in the mail. He didn't realize it, but he had pushed me away after the first two months of our dating. He hung in there for the eight months, but he didn't deserve me. There was no way that I was going to settle. I knew that I had better move on because he was expecting wedding bells even though we were unhealthy for one another. His response to my text message was threatening. I knew not to ever contact him again.

Unconsciously, I again ran from one man into the arms of another. I started seeing a guy who was an acquaintance. We both didn't realize it, but his cousin worked at a company that I had resigned from. And the cousin knew Paige my old friend from a former job—who had tricked me with the casting company fake offers. Without realizing it, I was out on a search trying to find my future husband. I was matching up the answers and information I received from the psychic.

But I gave no thought to evaluating what this new man in my life was saying, and I wasn't taking things slowly. I never followed up on my own to confirm whether or not he was telling the truth. He was filling my head with lies, financially broke, and working two jobs. He was also grieving the death of his mother. I showed him some emotional support while he was dealing with the pain. We were both rebounds, and he had been previously engaged. Overall, I was his short fling, and I got upset with him after he decided to go back to his fiancée. He wanted to string me along until he was sure that he was back in good with her. He even had the nerve to ask if he could come back one day if we both were single. I told him no; he had played with my emotions and was emotionally unstable.

This fling brought me to a screeching halt. I was going through the emotions of someone desperate for a man. I didn't know my true value or self worth, and I was afraid of being alone. I cried many nights, feeling lost and stupid for trusting somebody else to treat me right. The devil was whispering evil things in my ear. I cried out to God to stop the pain. He came to me one night, called my name, and told me to have faith.

My "new year" in 2002 continued to spiral. My mask wasn't working that well; people could see that something was wrong. Yes, I was terrified and afraid to move forward. I couldn't shake feeling awful, torn apart, and in despair. I needed God more than ever in my life. The devil would often tell me that I had messed up, and he also told me that I might as well get out there and do my own thing. But I told him that he was a liar. I was not going to turn my back on God unless He turned His on me. I went on a seven-day prayer consecration. Each day I would pray with a friend at six a.m. and at nine p.m. I was determined to hear God speak or work in my life to alleviate the pain.

One evening I needed to pray, but I couldn't find anyone available. So I called Jacob to my room, and I asked him to pray for me. I will never forget the beautiful words that he spoke to God. His words brought joy to my heart. I also kept a daily journal, in which I recorded that "...on the fifth night an angel appeared to me." I woke up, and the angel was staring at me. I closed my eyes while I began to pray, and it disappeared. I made up my mind to start walking with the Lord and praying to seek His Kingdom.

On the morning of January 23rd, which happened to be Jacob's birthday, the telephone rang while I was getting dressed for work. My granddaddy had died. He had lived to be ninety-one years old. My heart became heavier as I made room to carry this additional pain. I went home to Alabama to pay my respects and show my thankfulness. He was the only man in my life who had never harmed me. His love and actions were pure. I will never forget this man, Bishop Jonathan A. Wakefield, Sr. I have my granddaddy's spirit, and I know that God placed me in his care at an early age to protect my soul for the plans that He had bestowed upon my life. *"For I know the thoughts that I think toward you"*, says the LORD, *"thoughts of peace and not of evil, to give you a future and a hope."* (Jeremiah 29:11)



The bus ride back to Illinois gave me some time to think after seeing my granddaddy lying there in that casket. I reminisced about how my father had looked when I read his father's obituary. I didn't know if he had ever been proud of me, and I felt completely lost in the world. But the pain that I was feeling from my past relationships had started to subside, and my life was changing as I grew closer to God and His Word. Months ago I had only retaliation on my mind, and my heart was full of rage. I shared a lot of my pain with a cousin we called "Chop." She had always been there for me during late nights we shared deep conversation. She would tell me how good God was to me, because I seemed to get into one mess after another. And He would rescue me every time. She also inspired me to write this book about my life story, and she gave me the title, *Rhythm of Rage*. I've been abused, rejected, and unloved from the first day I arrived here on earth. The majority of my mistakes were due to trusting someone else to love me. I have battled with a spirit of rage. I became a victim to it, and I allowed certain circumstances to get inside my mind to cause harm. But because

I was taught about Jesus early in my life, I learned to give Him the chance to work in my life.

Chop brought me back to reality, enabling me to reevaluate myself by looking at how my life had been. This inspired me to keep fighting for what I couldn't see that lay ahead. She would reiterate that all pain isn't put into your life to destroy you, but it is to make you stronger, especially if it brings you closer to God. "*And we know that all things work together for good to those who love God, to those who are the called according to His purpose.*" (Romans 8:28). I mailed a letter to one of my aunt's pastors, whom I had previously met. I thanked him for his prayers and support at that particular time. The letter disclosed what I was petitioning to God—the battles I was trying to overcome. Shortly after, I dreamed I was inside a house. And as I was leaving, I saw a man standing in the door with a white piece of paper in his hands. He said that I could have all the things I had written about in my letter, but that I wasn't ready yet. I knew that God was speaking to me.

I kept a journal of all of the things that God was revealing, and I started searching for a church to fellowship close to home. Springtime was in the air, and God had wiped away all my tears. I started feeling hopeful again about life. I had a lot to be thankful for, regardless of how I was feeling, because the Lord had been mighty good.

In my search for a church, I knew that I had to find a Bible teaching church that believed in God the Father, Jesus the Son, and the Holy Sprit. I found a Pentecostal church that J.R. had been invited to attend with a schoolmate a long time ago. There was something different about this church that I enjoyed. The service and the atmosphere were very pleasant. When church let out, I always left immediately. But this church had a newcomer's luncheon that I decided to attend. I felt that I could find out more details about its doctrine and principles. At the luncheon, I started reading some materials. When I looked up, there was a tall brother asking if he could sit at my table. He introduced himself as Shamir, and we had a small conversation. He started by saying that he'd been looking for a wife since 1996. I told him to be patient and wait on God. My spirit started to change because my flesh started rising. And then I turned away from him while I rebuked my flesh. I wasn't trying to hear what this brother was saying. When the luncheon was over, on my way out the door, I heard the pastor asking this man if he had found a job.

On Father's Day I was at church, and I went over to the bookstand as I realized that I knew the lady who sold the books. She had a Christian bookstore in a town where I used to live. I remember talking to her about the Lord a few years back. We chatted for a moment. And when I turned around, Shamir was standing on my right. He asked if he could sit with me during service. He was dressed as though he had an interview of some kind. I believe it was a part of his plan to win my attention. He was trying to talk during the service by writing notes. He gave me his number, and I gave him my hotmail address. After service let out, he wanted to have a brief conversation. He confessed that he was a recovering addict, and I immediately felt that I didn't want any part of that life. The smile on my face dropped. People were coming over to talk to him about the service and to fellowship. I could see that he was well-liked by the members. A man with his stature and build drew a lot of attention. That's when I went to leave, but Shamir stalled me in the parking lot.

During the following week I was struck by another driver coming head-on. But by the grace of God, just before I was hit, I saw the other car driving towards me out of the corner of my eye. I couldn't prevent what seemed inevitable. There was no time for fear or a second to blink. It felt unreal as though I was watching a cartoon. It happened the morning of June 27th at the corner by my office. When I heard the loud collision noise, I began to call on the name of Jesus. He brought my car to a stop in the middle of the four-way intersection. I made it out of the car alive, and I started thanking God once I made it safely to the ground. The other driver was knocked unconscious, but she survived also.

My car was totaled, and I went on medical leave. I was blessed to have survived the wreck without any crushed or broken bones. And I had been wearing my seatbelt. I contacted all of my associates and personal contacts via e-mail about my accident. While I was resting at home one afternoon, I received a phone call from Shamir. He said he got my number through directory assistance. He vowed not to call again. I was in shock and disbelief that I didn't have my number unlisted. I also realized that he knows where I live. I was pissed, and it was revealed in the tone of my voice.

Later when I was resting in bed, my doorbell rang. It was a florist delivering some flowers from the church. Shamir had informed the church about my accident during weekly prayer. I was feeling isolated because I had no one who genuinely wanted to be there without an ulterior motive. I felt all alone. I had received some help here and there, but it wasn't the same as knowing I was being cared for because I was loved. That got me down as I started to reevaluate my life again; even so, I knew that God was there the whole time.

Eventually I went back to work part-time. I had to depend on my son and Saul's help to get back and forth. The Sunday that I returned to the church was also the day of the Annual Picnic. When service dismissed, I was encouraged to stay for the food. When I spotted Shamir lifting some chairs, he looked different. I could tell that he had lost weight. The Holy Spirit put in my spirit that he was using drugs again, but I wasn't sure that it was the Holy Spirit warning me. Still, I felt that something wasn't right about him. I sat around and talked to several people, and eventually he came over to where I was sitting to talk.

On my next visit to church, as I was leaving to go home, Shamir stopped me. He wanted to show me his achievements and memoirs. He said that he had accomplished more than the average person in his or her life, and he felt that I hadn't believed him when he'd mentioned it at the picnic. Then he asked me how I was going to get to know him if I kept running. I told him that I didn't trust him, and he replied that I could trust him better than myself. He was quite confident to make such a statement, I felt. I told him that I was waiting on my ex to pick me up, but he said that it didn't intimidate him.

While we were standing outside talking, Saul drove up. I introduced both men, and they each said that they had seen the other somewhere before. When I got home, Shamir called. And I could tell that he was beating around the bush. He went on to say that he had met Saul at a place I would never go. Then he said he seen Saul talking to a girl he knew. I didn't care. I believed that Shamir was trying to size up my life. After that phone conversation, we did continue to email each other.

It was late summer, and I wanted to get out and enjoy the weather. I went for my usual walks around the lake. One afternoon I decided to give Shamir a call on my cell phone. He jumped at the opportunity to hang out, and he brought this huge trash bag full of papers. He had newspaper articles, pictures in the press, certificates, and check stubs. He was trying to impress me with paper because his current situation wasn't adding up. As his phone calls continued, however, I gave in. And I went to dinner with him. After dinner he called me and said, "Let's get married so that we don't have to lust or sin." I countered by saying that the Bible says, *"Be anxious for nothing, but in everything by prayer and supplication, with thanksgiving, let your requests be made known to God; and the peace of God, which surpasses all understanding, will guard your hearts and minds through Christ Jesus."* (Philippians 4:6-7).

Shamir was working part-time. I told him that my kids didn't know him, and that I couldn't do anything intimate without knowing him. We started spending more time together after church on Sundays. He would compliment me by saying that I was attractive, humorous, ambitious, rich with wisdom, and that he loved my smile. These were the kind of words that a woman loves to hear. He would say he was very picky when he chose the type of woman that he wanted to be with. But he had known the day he saw me walking into the church that he had to marry me. He offered to take the boys and me out to eat after church, but J.R. declined. Shamir had met both my kids at church before the car accident. J.R. was still hopeful that maybe his father and I would get back together someday, and he felt that Shamir was a buster.

In the past my son and I had had a big disagreement when he refused to give me any support when Alexius betrayed me. I was trying to get him to see how manipulative she could be, but she had brainwashed him. She told him that I deserved it because I had "done her wrong." He was torn between us; he couldn't see through her lies. That whole issue brought division between us. It was devastating that she could get into the mind of my child to manipulate him. When I expressed my pain to the wrong people, they enjoyed throwing it in my face. These people questioned whether my son had any love for me. It was painful, but I had to trust God to work things out.

When J.R. came over to visit, Shamir would leave. He was not comfortable around my son after he'd declined the offer to dinner. Shamir was also not happy with me telling my business to my "so-called" friends. He was trying to persuade me to stop it. Shamir was sharing some of his own life's lessons. It did make sense; I knew that some people enjoyed hearing about my failures and watching my drama like the soaps on TV. Shamir had accompanied me to several outings, and he had the opportunity to see who my "fake" friends were. He approached everyone with a kind demeanor as though he was helping, and he knew how to be smooth about it. I felt that what he speculated was correct. He said that he had a PhD in the streets. He could read you by body language, eyes, handshake, etc.—and he was absolutely on the money a majority of the time.

There was some truth to what Shamir had speculated because I had always confided in Chop about my friends. There were times when

I would be very upset after being burned and hurt. Her advice also was to let these people go because they weren't my true friends, and they were in my life to use me. Shamir suggested that I find a new set of friends, so I started pulling away from my usual circle. Even so, I felt that I had to do more cleaning. The space I used to have for my friends was now being occupied by Shamir.

On Labor Day weekend after church, we both met with the pastor about premarital advice. He told Shamir to allow God to bring us together and to not force the situation. After that talk we went to the mall, and he decided to put an engagement ring on layaway. It was a beautiful ring, but very costly. He wasn't listening to what the pastor had suggested because he said that God told him that I was his wife. I told him that God said I wasn't ready yet. I stressed that I needed time to heal, but Shamir wasn't listening. I was in doubt because he didn't have a stable job with benefits, and his past was in question. We had several battles that went back and forth about him feeling as if I was taking my "baggage" out on him. He threw this in my face to get me to soften up to give him a chance. I admitted that I had issues from the beginning as to my reason for not being ready. I had a wall up because I knew that I couldn't take a chance on being hurt again—and especially not that soon. Still, he was ignoring what I was saying because he was determined to have me.

Shamir started convincing me that we would make a great team especially since we had met in the church. He said if God's word was true regarding forgiveness, then how could I look at his past mistakes when everybody had some? He said he wasn't looking for a woman to live with, but one that he couldn't live without. He would also give me this speech about, *"I don't need you when I'm doing well."* He was struggling from a deficit and needed help to get back on track. I gave in and started helping him with his resume, and I tried to be more supportive.

We set a date in December to marry, though I told him only if it was God's will. We didn't file for the marriage license because I still wasn't feeling it. I was praying and asking God for a sign. So I put out a fleet, requesting that God prevent Shamir from being hired if He didn't want me to marry him. Shamir's part-time job was ending because it was seasonal, so I had referred him to a company. I knew a business owner, Tim, that I thought would employ him. I had great confidence as I knew this lead could turn into something positive, based on my referral, and, of course, his credentials.

Shamir's feedback after meeting Tim was positive. He said that Tim had talked like he could use him, but he couldn't pay him what he was worth. Due to Shamir's outstanding credentials, Tim was willing to give him some part-time work and be flexible when he needed to take off for interviews. Well, we waited for a call from Tim, but it never came. Shamir started working the midnight shift at a retail chain. He was frustrated because he felt that he was above it, and he complained about having back problems. In the meantime I started to get worried because December was approaching, and I needed to make that decision. I didn't want to make a mistake. Shamir started reminding me that I had promised him, and that it wasn't fair. I reminded Shamir that he had made me promise him that commitment. Then I apologized, but I insisted that we couldn't get married under these circumstances. So he put on the love talk, and he asked me if I loved him. I told him "yes," but love doesn't pay the bills. I told him that he needed a job with benefits. So I set another date in April. A friend said that a job wasn't too hard for God if that was all Shamir needed. It was encouraging to know that God could help him, but regardless I wasn't going to marry him without a permanent full time job. I didn't fully trust him. Additionally, I had always had my doubts about his past. Something wasn't right.

Saul, who was still up to his evil schemes, enjoyed causing hell in my life. He called to say he was going to take me to court to get custody of Jacob. He was wicked and very unhappy, so he wanted me to feel the same way. I got so tired of being stressed by other folks' negativity that I put a restraining order against Saul. I realized that it was all about the money with him. He wanted me to pay him child support.

I concluded that I needed to find a way to get my life back on track, but I didn't know how to resolve my issues. I caught the bus to Laredo, Texas, for Christmas 2002 to visit a friend. The bus ride was long, and the landscape was quite different. It felt like I had passed by all my stops; I ended up being the only African American on the bus that spoke English. When I saw the palm trees, they reminded me of California. The weather was sunny and beautiful. I stayed in a little town called Cotula, which had approximately two African Americans in the whole town. I was definitely in the country because I could hear the rooster's crowing in the morning.

The town natives spoke Spanish as their primary language. There were many vacant buildings and homes. Poverty was very apparent, and life seemed to be moving in slow motion. I forgot to not drink the water, and I got sick for a few days. During one sunny afternoon, my girlfriend and I planned to go shopping in Mexico. I asked her plenty of questions before we left. In order to enter Mexico, you had to pay a fee. I felt tense while I was putting my change into the coin machine to cross over the border. The Mexican police stood out in the streets with their Uzis fully loaded. It was frightening to see how poverty had stricken so many lost souls. Once I crossed back over into the United States, I prayed and thanked God for watching over my soul.

Once I made it safely back home, Shamir was determined to throw it in my face that I had gone across the border without a visa. He was furious because my cell phone hadn't been getting clear reception. I was more concerned that Shamir's job had ended, and he had been presented with other possibilities in management that he had declined. He had found another job through the temp service that had a greater chance of becoming permanent, and I noticed a difference in his personality each time he was working—how cocky he'd act! He made it clear as though he was doing it for me. I was dealing with his attitude, issues, and anger, which I identified as the syndrome of the "Angry Black Man."

The temp job didn't work out and spring came. There was no harmony in my life with Shamir as the center of attention. He didn't get along with my kids, because Saul was against us. Shamir was very frustrated by my boy's behavior, and he bickered constantly about them. I began to tell him that we were not going to make it. Then he would blow up in my face. I told him that my kids and I were a package deal. Finally, we agreed to go see the assistant pastor about our relationship. Shamir coached me about what to refrain from disclosing in our meeting. We didn't talk about our sins because Shamir didn't want anyone judging us. I partially agreed, believing that only God should be the one to judge. But, of course, Shamir had a motive behind everything. I believe the reason he wanted to do this was to keep me confused so that I would submit to marrying him.

The assistant pastor said that Shamir was a diamond in the rough, and even though he had a lot of growing to do in Christ; he felt that Shamir was trying. He wanted to help us, but it was going to take some commitment on both our parts.

Shamir didn't care as long as he foresaw us getting married. A few weeks later, we went to get our marriage license and some cheap rings. I felt like I had let myself down, and I had fallen back into the pit. I didn't want to continue doing things this way. I tore up the marriage license into tiny little pieces. I was battling with conviction and how to get back on track with my walk with the Lord.

Summer came before we knew it. Shamir finally got hired to do what he'd boasted about doing the whole entire time. He started work as a senior V.P. of logistics. He said I didn't believe in him, and he got a big head. He boasted about how his life was going to soar. He still presented marriage, but he said it would be on his terms this time. Supposedly he was still making payments on my first ring, but it really didn't matter to me at this time. He was changing, but I couldn't really see the full picture. He was scaring me. One day he went off at me, and he started using profanity. My feelings were deeply hurt, which caused me to back away. He was letting me know that he was the boss, and his conversations changed from talking about professional things to people who smoked drugs. He knew who was using them in the community and on the job. He had talked about these things in the past, but he'd start off with how good God was to him. Shamir shared his desire to stay clean and sober.

When he received his first paycheck, he repaid money that he owed me. And he showed integrity by taking steps to make amends to those who had been there for him. I decided to talk about marriage again because I thought that maybe he was going to keep this job. I felt that it gave him some self-esteem and confidence to be independent again.

On Shamir's next payday, he went "missing in action" that evening. I called his cell phone, and another man answered. I panicked and hung up the phone. Immediately I felt weak and frightened in my spirit. I was reliving parts of my past all over again, but even worse. The Holy Spirit revealed to my spirit that Shamir was on drugs, plain and clear. I was thinking various thoughts at this time because his sister-in-law had just passed away, and we were planning to attend the funeral the next day. I dialed his cell at least three times within the hour, and the same guy always answered. Eventually Shamir called from his job to check in. I asked him where he was, and he said he was hanging out with the boys. He said that he'd only had a beer. I knew that meant trouble because his friends were all a part of his negative past. He had expressed how they were bad for him, and he could never trust them. I knew that his frame of mind had changed now, and the change could only be caused by drugs.

When he came over, I told him I wanted us to part. He snapped, threatening to throw me off the balcony. My heart fell deep into my chest, and then I started praying under my breath. Shamir went on to tell me how I held him back, and he could have been married several times as there were other women interested in him. I started having flashbacks that confirmed what all that hesitation and being leery was all about. It was the Holy Spirit trying to warn me. I remembered the vision in the dream that God had revealed before I met Shamir: the next test that I had to face. I knew that I wasn't ready yet for marriage because God had spoken it to me in my dream.

It was very frightening as I tried to calm him down, but he went on and on for hours. I was definitely afraid for my life; no one was around to intervene. Everything had shattered right in front of my face. After everything hit the fan, I knew that I had to get away from him. He kept calling to feed me more lies to buy more time. I gave him back everything I had of his, and I told him to keep whatever he owed me. He kept saying that he was a good man, and he had only messed up once. I said I was sure I was done with him, and I explained that I was going to get some counseling.

He started talking very nasty. He was saying demeaning things. Eventually I got my phone number changed, but he started calling my job and leaving voicemails. He left several messages about worldly things saying that this was a "Tupac and Biggie Smalls" issue now. He even brought a nasty letter to my job and left it with the receptionist. I was terrified, and I didn't know what to do. One time he left a voice message saying that he liked the way I moved the furniture around in my apartment. I wasn't worried about it because I had renter's insurance, and I had the locks changed. But his behavior escalated to the point that I had to get other people involved. When I got home, I went to my neighbor's apartment to ask her to walk with me up to mine. She was very supportive as we went up the stairs from the front. He had left nasty notes on each stairway, and he had written on the walls with a marker and on my apartment door. He also wrote nasty language on the wall in the laundry room. Once I got into my apartment, I was relieved because he hadn't broken into it. Then I called the police. I also called J.R. and told him some of the news. I didn't want him to do anything crazy out of haste. But J.R. told Saul, and that was all it took to get things "riled up" between them. Shamir had made some threatening comments about the kids, which made Saul furious. Saul was determined to have a word with him. He demanded that I give him Shamir's number. The two of them went back and forth cussing each other out.

The next day I went to court to file a restraining order against Shamir. He called my work, and he left more threatening voicemails. By this time he was really ticked off at me for giving Saul his phone number. Little did I know that the both of them had arranged to fight at the gas station near my house. Saul had his girlfriend drive him over to the gas station while he waited for Shamir to show up. Saul had Jacob and his girlfriend's children in the van with them! While all of this was going on, my doorbell rang. When I asked who it was, no one answered. I sensed that it was Shamir. When the doorbell rang again ten minutes later, this time it was Saul. After I buzzed him up, he explained what was happening. He asked me if Shamir had been over. I told him about the doorbell ringing ten minutes earlier. We both assumed it was him. I was praying that no one got hurt or murdered, because Saul is a nut all by himself.

The morning after I woke, I called Shamir's mother to explain to her what was going on. She was saddened to hear what her son was doing, and she contacted him to ask him to stop acting that way. She knew that I was a decent person. I allowed his mother and family to listen to his threatening voicemails because I knew of no other way to get him to back off and stop this madness.

Once I got to work my desk phone light was red. I dreaded checking my voicemail for fear of what might be next. I had approximately thirteen new messages, and they all were from Shamir. He stated on one message that he had rung my doorbell. And then he went on to say all kinds of hateful things, threatening to go to my old friends, and tell them our secrets.

I had to find some solitude. I went into a deep thought as I analyzed my relationship with him. He had been eager for me to meet his mom and family because they lived a decent and normal life, which he knew would make a good impression on him.

The last voicemail that I received from Shamir was an apology. I avoided his calls because I knew a way to call him back without speaking directly to him. I left a voicemail, and I sent him an e-mail to express my sorrow, hurt, and feelings of betrayal. That was the last of the manipulation, lies, traps, and deceit that he used to try to destroy my soul and mind.

I cried endlessly for many days and nights about my mistakes and choices. I searched for scriptures to help me because I believe that everything happens for a reason. As I made it through the storms, I built courage, hope, and faith in God, not man. As I looked within I was seeking resolution. In my finite, little mind I reasoned that God had never sent Shamir to be my husband because his spirit wasn't right. God stepped in to show me that vision about the letter and the man in the house. God put in my spirit these four words: "I'm not ready yet." He knew that this test was coming, and He wanted me to learn to listen to His voice within. I was that little sheep that had fallen into the pit. I never stopped praying and crying out to God for refuge.

Shamir had made his own choices, which were reflected in his life. He wanted me to walk that walk with him. He had seen my walk with the Lord, and he hoped that I would be that anchor while he fought with his demons and battled his addiction. But he had never loved me or appreciated the things that I did for him because he wasn't delivered. There's an old saying that true colors will come out in the wash.

God was with me all the time, and nobody can tell me differently. What doesn't destroy you, will definitely make you stronger. I have learned more in the past year than I have in my entire life. When I look at the good that God has done, my soul cries out *hallelujah* to God for saving me. All that pain wasn't meant to destroy me, but it was to elevate me to the next level that God had prepared. Satan can't harm a hair on my head without God's permission.

Since then, I have moved on with my life. And I have more peace. I have a better relationship with my sons and a greater appreciation for my freedom. It's a battle to stay free and untangled as I continue to seek the Lord for my destiny. I realize that He isn't going to allow me to go forth until I start walking in the direction that He has planned. I got the courage to pick up the pen, and I have continued to write. I started where I left off a year ago—before this nightmare walked into my life. As I allow the Holy Spirit to teach me the unsearchable things of God, I hold onto believing that God loves me in spite of my mess. Pain will teach you many things. And I've learned that when you have a spiritual calling, nothing will start to make sense in the natural until you start to grow in the spiritual things of God.

# CHAPTER 10

As time went on, the healing process was taking place. I felt that I needed to move to clear my thoughts and to do things differently. It was, of course, God's will because things began to happen supernaturally in my life. Doors were being open that seemed shut, and favor was pouring down upon my soul. One afternoon while I was on my break at work, I called my cousin, Nella. I needed prayer. Nella made a three-way call to include another prayer warrior. Sister Hopewell started praying. Then she suddenly spoke about things that only God knew that were happening with me. I felt some deep encouragement after I got off the phone. The next morning was Saturday. While I was sleeping, I heard a strong voice say, "I will create in you a new spirit." I lied still with my eyes closed. Then I opened my eyes, and I looked up at the ceiling. I instantly knew that it was God, as I reminisced about the day before.

I didn't quite know what that meant, but I recall reading something in the Bible regarding a right spirit and a renewed creature. I felt amazed as I climbed out of bed. I contacted Sister Hopewell to pray again. I listened intently while she spoke with boldness. I knew what God wanted me to do. So, I remained quiet because I was still unsure. I devoted more time to seek clarity and an answer from God.

On another occasion during a phone conversation I had with Sister Hopewell, she asked me to send her one of my writings. I didn't know what she was referring to. As I contemplated about what she was asking for I got down on my knees, and I looked underneath my bed and reached for some poems that I had written a while back. I blew the dust off the wrinkled pages, and I read one of them. I immediately sent her one in the form of a bookmark. I felt that was the least I could do for her taking the time out of her day to pray for me. The day that the package arrived sister Hopewell called. She was touched by the words. I was honored and so amazed to hear such compliments coming from a stranger. She begins prophesizing more things about how God was going to use me. During this time I was seeking a closer relationship with God. There was something about this woman that compelled me to stay in contact with her, because I had major issues with trusting people and even myself. Prior to this connection I had shut down, because I knew of no one that could help me.

Shortly after that phone call to Sister Hopewell during April 2004, I began to dream dreams and see visions in my sleep. The Lord began to show me pages of writings, and the words were in cursive. It was vivid. He began to whisper softly to my spirit throughout the following days and nights different titles of what to write. I remained in touch with sister Hopewell to testify how real God was by showing me these things.

I became compassionate to the point that I couldn't hold it inside me anymore. I shared the inspirations with fellow acquaintances at work. I put them in bookmarks, and I gave them out to strangers, family and friends. I received positive feedback from almost everyone that I contacted. I was presented with different ideas of what I could do with them. Those were the seeds that gave me the inspiration to remain faithful to writing. A co-worker copied a tape of an inspiring speech by a world renowned speaker Earl Nightingale, "The Strangest Secret." I received it with great anticipation and appreciation. I couldn't wait to get home and settled into bed that evening to listen to it. I became addicted to following Earl's thirty-day program. The requirement was to think positive thoughts for thirty days. If you start to think negative, you had to start all over again and count from there as day one. Earl's philosophy states "what a man thinks about, that is what he becomes." I listened intently to receive the best results. I even wrote down my goals pertaining to my new path. I envisioned everything that the Lord was revealing to my spirit. I had started a dream journal previously, in 2002. As time went on, I would add new information. I had an epiphany of what I wanted more than ever in my life. I wanted to continue to hear God's voice and please him with all my heart. I also wanted to be happy and have the blessings that were prophesied about my life. After the thirty days, I didn't understand the next step to attracting positivity into my life. I began to feel this surge of energy within me. It was slowly progressing as I went on about my day. I was mesmerized about how good I felt. I remember going home from work to lie down on my bed. Numerous thoughts crossed my finite mind. On the next day, I was at my desk when this force of energy rose within me enabling me to feel stronger. I paused and took a deep breath. And I placed my hand over my heart to count the rapid beating. I felt a warmth running up and down inside. At that point I bowed my head. I turned my face away to avoid anyone seeing how I was blushing. I needed to talk to someone. I didn't want my co-workers to think that I was cracking up or having an illusion of some sort. I called a co-worker from a different department to meet me in the cafeteria. We met, and I begin to tell him about my experience. As I sat there in view of my co-worker, I contemplated about how I was feeling. Immediately, I started blushing. I rambled for the right words to say. I told him that I believed that God was doing something spiritual within me. He was patient and quiet while listening to me. As we started talking, he related to me some of his experiences with the Lord. He started quoting scriptures. Our conversation was an affirmation, because the scripture he spoke about was Habakkuk 2:2, letting me know that this was a confirmation to manifesting the things that I believe God can do. It was an unforgettable and powerful experience. I knew that I was on the right path, and my mind was healthy to succeed. I learned that I had to be careful to whom I disclosed my dreams and experiences with. Sometimes people are naturally negative about something that they have no experience with or very little knowledge about. I learned to pay attention to my intuition.

Eight months after living in my new apartment, in December 2004, the Lord started dealing with me regarding my father. I had several conversations about him with people who understood my vision. I asked the Lord many questions about what He was trying to tell me. I felt that I had always opened the door of communication with my father whenever I had seen him. He had asked for forgiveness over fifteen years ago, and I forgave him. But I was puzzled about the fact that he hadn't reached out to me since then, and I asked the Lord why He was allowing me to think about my father this much. This weighed heavy on my heart because I felt like the prodigal daughter. I cried over this during the questioning period. I felt that the Lord loved me, and I had forgiven Jonathan—so why weren't things different?

Shortly after sharing my feelings I had a dream about Jacob, my son, dying. In this dream, I was sitting in a church attending his funeral with Amaris, my godsister, who was also deceased. When I awoke, I prayed to the Lord and spoke about this to a few people. I immediately thought about Jacob, who was away at his dad's during the holiday break. I couldn't reach either of my sons by phone. I calmed down and said, "Lord, they are yours first before they're mine." Eventually J.R. called my work on the third day. He said that their phone ringer had been turned on low. I was relieved more than anything because I knew that Saul would have contacted me if anything serious had happened.

The following day at work, I received a message to call my cousin concerning a family emergency. I prolonged returning the phone call for about two hours because I wanted to finish the month-end report. I knew that my mind wasn't going to be right after I returned the call. Also, it was the last working day of the year. Then I slipped away into a conference room to make the call. My father had died that morning.

As I began to cry, I felt the big empty loss of his love. And it was too late to ever have it. I had wanted him to love me. I had struggled with this for a whole month. I asked the Lord to help me with this issue. I had my times of reliving the fear of my father's abuse, but as I matured in Christ I knew that it was the devil that made his flesh do those mean things. I held dear to the memories of the times when he was good to me.

While I was pondering and reminiscing about those good days, I had a smile on my face because I knew that I had made the right decision in forgiving Jonathan. I wanted to live my life peacefully so that God could bless me; that's why I surrendered that hurt to Him. I knew it wasn't my job to avenge the hurt, which only makes the scar worse. I must forgive in order to be forgiven for my sins. Time does heal all wounds. I'm a living witness of it. I wrote a poem to my father called, "I Pray," in which I expressed how I am that innocent seed that God had placed in his life, to protect and care for until I grew into a beautiful flower. In spite of everything, I loved him no matter what storms came because I was a reflection of something good that happened in his life.

On my journey to Alabama for the funeral, I wrestled with many thoughts. I didn't know how to feel about the reunion with Rocky and Lionel. We would all grow in our own ways in life, and we had to learn how to cope with our abusive childhood. My spirit affirmed that I had to face this mountain and have closure in this chapter of my father's life. I prayed and asked the Lord to prepare me, to purge my thoughts, and make my heart humble and acceptable in His sight.

When I got to Alabama, I took pictures of the house that my great grandfather had built in the late eighteen hundreds. I had lived in this house in 1979 when I moved to Alabama. When I first saw the house I remembered how ashamed of it I was. Twenty years had passed since I had graduated from high school and left Wakefield Hill. These were pictures taken for the first time. What I saw was humble beginnings. This was where I had learned the most about the legacy of hard work from working in the fields, caring and feeding the animals, sitting with the elderly, and looking at the world in a different way. I saw the beauty of nature and how everything in life must change. The red dirt road that led up to Wakefield Hill was paved with cement, and I reminisced about Highway 219 when I saw the signs. Visiting Wakefield Hill brought back memories of my youth when the sun shone and the rainstorms that would follow—sometimes in the same day. We would all get inside this three-room house and sit still—listening to the Lord move his furniture around in heaven. The sounds from the rain that fell on the tin roof made for the best sleep a person could dream of.

This is a photograph of my great grandfather Wills' house built in the late 1800's. This photo was taken January 2005.

I walked the land and took pictures of the hillside as I prayed and asked God to keep me humble. I can see that this was a part of His plan for my life; this was the place that had shaped me into the woman that I am today. I was thankful because I had come from dirt to praise!

God is an awesome God. I just love Him so much for not giving up on me, for knowing the whole purpose to my life. I'm crying as I type this chapter because no one knows how my heart feels after enduring a life of ongoing pain and hurt. It's not easy to do the right thing all the time when you have to walk alone. I think of the scripture in the Bible that says, *God will never leave you nor forsake you.* That has been proven in all my years of living on this planet called Earth.

When I reunited with Rocky, he embraced me with a big hug while we both smiled. I was shocked to see that he had aged greatly in the past ten years since our last meeting. I tried to mask what I was feeling inside at that moment. I could see the joy that he had in his eyes because we both were still alive. I met my niece and nephew, who were seven and eight years old, for the first time; and joy filled my heart. I gave them both big hugs and smiled. I didn't know their real names at first, but everyone called them "Pancake" and "Cornbread." As I wandered back down memory lane, I could see that they resembled Rocky and me when we were little.

Unfortunately, Lionel was again unable to attend this union. I did unite with one of my half sisters and my other niece, whom I hadn't seen for ten years. I had the chance to slip away the night before the funeral to view the body. I placed the poem that I had written inside Jonathan's pants pocket. While riding back to my family's house, I was quiet. As I stared into the night, I felt fear being released from me. I no longer had to fear my past.

Rocky and I buried our father, and we grieved in our own ways. He had been found in a praying position, so I believe that my father is with the Lord. He was raised in the truth, and we both shared the same upbringing by the late Jonathan A. Wakefield Sr. My father was a very handsome, warm spirited, humble, friendly kind of guy. He had plenty of stories to tell, and he would be smiling, laughing, and shaking his head. It was as though he was reliving his life and expressing his gratefulness to God almighty. He was very rich in wisdom; he had dynamic carpentry skills and a way of fixing anything that was broken out of scraps. He had inherited all these talents and good looks from his dad. But one thing was for sure: he never wanted to be a preacher. But the Lord made sure he was ready in one form or another.

In conclusion, my dad was that rough edge that taught me to forgive and to love. Satan used him during his years of drinking and drugging to try to destroy me so that I couldn't reach my purpose. It was a big test. I had a choice to be resentful or evil because of the pain he caused me. But instead I looked to the hills for my refuge.

While reflecting and looking within, I reevaluated my life. I removed my shadow of a mask to where I stand today. I have an inner peace that exudes. I no longer hunger for superficial things or love. I'm stronger, wiser, and in tune with knowing the difference in how I feel when my life is calm and healthy versus when I was agitated and living unhealthy. Everything that I have experienced, and the choices that I made were ordained. I was shaped by the many circumstances that happened to me. However, now that I am born again, I have experienced true joy and love with God. Once upon a time when I was alone, I thought I was lonely and needed something or someone to fill that void. But oftentimes those opened unwanted doors led me astray. Since evolving, I've learned how to get quiet so that I can hear what God is saying by my intuition. I have a greater appreciation for the many things that I took for granted. These things are simple things such as making time to go for walks in the park, smiling when hearing laughter from the children outside, adoring the flowers that bloom, and stopping to smell the fresh air after new grass has been cut. I get excited when I see butterflies and a burst of energy while listening to the birds chirp in the morning. Before this transformation, I didn't understand how animated life really was. I was walking blind. Someday when my life comes to an end, I want to be one of those people who has a smile on their face and has no regrets to say the least about the things that hold such splendor.

As the air roamed softly through the wind during summer of 2005, I mustered the faith as I prepared for my first exhibit to introduce my inspirations to the world. There were several business entrepreneurs' setting up their booths and tables at the event. My table was decorated with sunflowers. I wanted to exude grace and tranquility to attract people. I did some networking, and I met a few inspiring people. I could feel the positive energy flowing from this one woman who took notice of my table. She bought a large quantity of bookmarks and frames, and she spoke words of inspiration. I was in awe and taken back to a year ago when all this began. As an act of faith I recall the Lord putting it into my spirit months earlier to write down a list of names. I obeyed and prayed over the list. Some time had passed by. I remember waking one morning, and I immediately picked up the list and chose the name "Reflections of Grace".

Reflections of Grace was founded in 2005. It is a spiritual inspirational writing company. This platform has given me a voice to inspire hope to others whose lives are in transition to a breakthrough. As I strive towards achieving my dreams, I will continue to follow the steps that God has planned. I realize that true peace and happiness comes from recognizing when you have a gift from God to share with all mankind to enlighten, enrich, and illuminate someone's journey.

As I leave work every day on my new journey, I drive down Schaumburg Road, but I've called it in my mind "Highway Heaven." While the cars are all lined up to go through the green light, I envision myself making one step in front of the other to be reunited with my Lord and Savior Jesus Christ. As I turn onto a road called Grace, I am truly grateful to see that God is with me. My mind, heart, soul, and spirit know that God will answer those who seek to know Him.

## HIGHWAY HEAVEN

You are on this journey without a tune-up
Sometimes you may grow weak and weary but faint not
Restoration and prayer are divine resources
Stay focused and in your lane

It doesn't matter when you get there
For the road is narrow
There will be detours, roadblocks and distractions
The ride does get bumpy

Watch for the signs; Jesus is directing the way
If you should stop to get help
Make sure you don't delay
Replenish what is needed and watch the speed limit

# THE LIGHT

As I travel towards the light
My soul cries for unquenchable joy
While my earthly cares seem to fade

Kindred spirits are in pursuit
There are many mysteries ahead
As I follow God's spirit

Nothing can hinder my steps
Through the piercing, storms and thorns
I have learned to press on

As I face each day
My spirit knows that time is passing
Therefore I can't look back on yesterday

My spirit is free as my soul sings
My mind is renewed through it all
Today I have another chance

As I make it through the gates of lights
I can scream and rejoice aloud
Because I believed in Gods' eternal word

# GOD THE AUTHOR



My life exists because of your will
I welcome your spirit to have its way
I pray to receive your word as I mature

I know in my heart that I belong to you
For my life is not my own
With that price I was given grace

When I made the wrong choices you forgave
I was blind and confused before I met you
Empty inside, but searching for love

You had your eyes on me the whole time
I cry because I realize that my life is not a mistake
You knew all along the plan

I understand that the world is not my friend
In you I have found everything even in my tears
I love you for being the author of my soul

# WOVEN WITHIN

While covered inside of my mother's womb
You knitted me out of mercy and grace
You spoke words to my spirit

I was made by your precious hands
To fulfill my purpose that you have planned
Your angels are watching over my life

Beautiful I am to have such a purpose
To come to earth to share with the world
The gift that you have planted inside my soul

Blessed I am to be woven within
I will cherish each day that I live to see
As I learn to use and devote my gift

# A GIFT

In the whole world the greatest gift to have
Are in the eyes of the beholder
When you find it don't let it go

A spiritual gift is one that possesses grace
To connect your soul to God above
Rejoice and share that awesome gift

Your life will become more fulfilled
What a divine and prosperous souvenir
As you flourish to use it blessings will flow

Give God the glory and praise
As you witness the wonders of His goodness
By sharing your spiritual gift

# A NEW SONG

As I write the melodies of God's heart
That He speaks to me with grace
What a joy I have to have found this gift

The words that we read in our life are stored
Way down inside of your soul that's where it is
In the quiet of times, or during the night

It replays the melodies that were placed inside
The notes and messages that you hear
Will reveal the secrets that's kept so deep

With praises and thanks for all of His mercies
My soul is dedicated to receive
The secrets that He breathes into my spirit

# AN ANGEL FOR ALL SEASONS



Time and time again I've wondered
About each road block that I've encountered
Some how the Lord made a way of escape

When I'm sick and can't get well
Here comes an angel to give me comfort
I pray to the Lord above for hearing my prayers

When I look back on my troubled life
I can say that there was an angel
Without God's special care I would be helpless

Oh my God you created such a wonderful gift
To share with all mankind
When you made heavenly angels to assist

# AN INSEPARABLE LOVE

Like the ocean that moves endlessly
I am mesmerized by your warmth
Day by day I am drawn

I pray to know you
There's something about your love
Souls are being connected through prayer

From the throne of grace your spirit rains
Words of compassion that comfort me
I'm nothing without you

Within my heart I believe
As the morning mist falls from heaven
I will praise you forever more

When I feel all alone
I will breathe and give my all
As I surrender to your love

# IN AWE

As your light shines upon the ocean
I will breathe and pray for grace
For your love is everlasting

When I rise please fill my soul
I can not live without your covering
Your sweetness surrounds my being

The power of your presence flows
While miracles are falling from above
My arms are open to embrace my portion

As your passion spreads all around
I'm elated to bow on my knees
Keep raining your mercy and goodness

There's an abundance I feel
Hallelujah I am in awe of heaven
As the wind blows

Lord I know that you live
I am grateful to show you my love
While I live to give you my praise

# A BUTTERFLY'S SPIRIT

Butterflies are a blessing
While the wind blows softly
My soul quivers at each ray

As God breathes life into my being
I am able to capture an awe of beauty
Within my spirit I am set free

The angels are rejoicing and singing
To everything that blooms
While butterflies learn to fly

To everything there is a season
As you rise and soar beyond mountains
God will grant His grace upon you

As butterflies appear expect a miracle
Reach out and speak life to your situation
While you witness Gods' blessings to others

# BEAUTY

You whisper sweet sounds to my mind
By allowing the birds to chirp outside
My soul rejoices when I see butterflies

God your beauty stands out among the stars
Rainbows appear after the storms
My eyes can not capture your love

Sweetness surrounds the flowers that bloom
All the colors of your love beholds your beauty
Seasons change to show your glory

My life depends on your grace and mercy
Endlessly you have given so much
As I live I thank you for sharing your love

# REJOICE

The aura of my soul will dance for you
As joy moves within my heart
I'm lost inside of your will

I see no tomorrow only what I feel
No time for sorrow and yes these tears are real
It's time to shout and give my praise

Hallelujah, joy sweet mercy
The love that I have for you is yours
Take all of me so I can receive

More of what I believe
To God be all the glory on earth
I feel that heaven must be rejoicing

As I kneel and pray to record this moment
There's no end to your beginning
Let the melodies play in my heart

# WHISPERS IN THE NIGHT

As I say my prayers to the Lord above
I wait for His anointing to fall upon my life
While my soul sleeps

I envision the blessings that He sends
While His angels sit by my side
What a joy to imagine

With mercy He whispers my name
Have faith and believe He speaks
My grace is sufficient for all your mistakes

During the midst of another sunrise
I opened my eyes
To give praise and thanks

As I reminisce about the prayers I prayed
Thank you Lord for opening my ears
To receive what the world can not hear

# SPIRIT OF GRACE

Upon my soul shines the light
As it beams from heaven
I know that its grace

Where ever I go on this journey
I can pray to God to be there
For I cannot capture His dimension

I tremble when trouble finds me
But my spirit calls out to thee
To release the chains of bondage

In my search to find my creator
I have learned to lean on His word
My eyes cannot see the evidence

But my spirit can rest assure
That His spirit and grace is with me
As He leads my soul to safety

# WITH MY SOUL

As I day dream about who I am
I know that there is a God that cares
In the midst of all my suffering and troubles

I've learned to escape when I pray
My heavenly father knows my name
Somehow He appears and resolves all my fears

When the storms are raging I run to Him
For He is my refuge and a powerful savior that lives
My soul knows that He's there

I believe that I am His with all my heart
And no matter what happens to my life
I am loved and that is well with my soul

"Lionel and I were shaking and crying because we didn't know what to do, and Rocky pulled out the Bible and read to us. Trying to comfort us he said, "If it isn't your time to die, then God won't take you." Then we heard our mother screaming, and falling as she tried to come up the stairs. When she called my name, "Naima!" I panicked. I was afraid to answer her—even when she started cussing and demanding that I go to her. Rocky said, "You better go." He unlocked the bedroom door to let me out. I went to the edge of the stairs. My mother saw my shadow and said, "Come here, heifer." When I went to her, she grabbed me and held me in front of her. We were standing halfway up the stairs on the landing, and Raymond was standing downstairs in the middle of the dining room. He was aiming his machine gun at us. Then he pulled the trigger. I could see the fire from the bullets coming straight at us. My mother and I screamed for him to stop. The bullets went by us and ricocheted into the ceiling above our heads. My mother and I ran upstairs to Rocky's room, and we jumped off the balcony to get outside alive."

- From Rhythm of Rage:
- The Story of Naima X

Made in the USA